Judy Puckett

GOD answers PRAYER

GREAT TESTIMONIES TO BUILD YOUR FAITH

GOD answers PRAYER

GREAT TESTIMONIES TO BUILD YOUR FAITH

COMPILED BY

MARY H. WALLACE

God Answers Prayer

compiled by Mary Wallace

Hazelwood, MO 63042
Printing History: 1986, 1996

Cover Design and Photography by Paul Povolni

All Scripture quotations in this book are from the King James Version of the Bible unless otherwise identified.

Printed in United States of America.

Printed by

WAP

Library of Congress Cataloging-in-Publication Data
Main entry under title:

God answers prayer.

1. Prayer. 2. Christian biography. 3. Christian life—Pentecostal authors.
I. Wallace, Mary H.
BV220.G59 1986 248.3′2 85-22484
ISBN 0-912315-90-3

Table of Contents

Author's Preface

When I sat down to write a short story about my father-in-law, J. W. Wallace, for the book *Profiles of Pentecostal Preachers,* I wanted to emphasize "Papa" Wallace's ministry of prayer to the sick. Ever since I had become a member of the Wallace family, I had heard marvelous stories of how Papa Wallace had prayed for the sick and God had healed. Healed of what? Where? When? These details which lend credibility to a story had faded from our memory since Papa's death in 1959.

"I will write down the details in the future," I promised myself. "I'll begin now." So I began to ask friends and associates for written, detailed accounts of how God had answered their prayers. "So that our children may hear the details and believe," I coaxed.

The stories began to arrive. Deliverance from a fire, a lost briefcase found, healing of cancer, a sandwich for a hungry Bible school student – big things, little things – but all things testifying to the miraculous, marvelous God of all comfort who hears and helps. "Hitherto hath the Lord helped us" (I Samuel 7:12). But by His grace there are even greater stories yet to be written. All these stories are true. Let faith rise in your heart as you read.

After you read these stories, if they remind you of times when God has answered your prayers, write the story down and send it to Pentecostal Publishing House, Editorial Department, 8855 Dunn Road, Hazelwood, Missouri 63042. We delight in hearing about the good things God has done and we may need to do another volume entitled *God Answers More Prayers.*

Foreword

God affords sufficient assurance that He is the same today as yesterday. Faithfulness is a part of His being. The infallibility of His Word further attests the consistency of the sameness of His power and character. Once God says something, it is forever truth.

God not only revealed that He was Jehovah Rapha, Jehovah Jireh, and Jehovah Tsidkeneu, but He confirmed it by His performance. Once a miracle is enacted it is forever available for repetition due to the fairness and justice of God's being.

Omniscience and omnipotence combined with perfect love and unending mercy provide indescribable and limitless potential.

What do you need? What do you desire? The Father's storehouse is overflowing with whatever we need. It is His good pleasure to supply His children's needs, which are already provided, paid for, purchased, waiting to be requested! There is an abundant supply "according to his riches in glory." How rich are His riches? Beyond our comprehension. Especially delighted is He to respond to all the needs of His little flock (See Luke 12:31, 32), even more than our desires (See Psalm 37:4; Mark 11:24) and more exceedingly, abundantly above all that we ask or think (Ephesians 3:20).

Since God in the beginning created thousands of stars by a spoken word and since He remains always the same, if we have a need, can He not supply it? Let us focus on the testimonies of present-day miracles—real names, actual experiences, and genuine people.

Marvelle Dees

CHAPTER ONE

Night Of Miracles

by Frances Vaughan

The night of April 26, 1984, is indelibly written in my memory. It affected each person in our community—for at 11:30 p.m. a tornado ripped through Morris, Oklahoma, leaving tons of rubble in its wake. It was over in two minutes. Seventy-five percent of our town was destroyed, seven people were killed, dozens were injured and hundreds were left homeless.

I was never afraid of storms. First of all, according to an old Indian legend, a tornado never touches down in this area because of the "lay of the land." Then the house we live in was built in 1904. When my husband, Dwaine, remodeled it, we pulled up mop-boards with the words MORRIS, INDIAN TERRITORY stenciled on the back. In tearing out partitions, we found two-by-fours without a single knothole and wood so hard we couldn't remove the nails. The old house had withstood many storms, so why should I worry?

Reasoning thus, I couldn't understand my anxiety as I lay in bed that night, listening to the rising wind. The air was so oppressive that I felt I would suffocate. I sat up, swinging my feet to the floor.

"What's the matter?" Dwaine asked, sleepily.

"It's so stuffy I can't breathe. I think I'll check the weather station," I answered, reaching for my robe.

Dwaine was instantly alert.

"I doubt if there is anything to be alarmed about," he said, grabbing his clothes. His quick actions belied his words.

Spinning the dial on the radio I found only the regular broadcasts.

Dwaine opened the front door, but the wind was so strong he quickly closed it.

The weather station on the scanner was still broadcasting a weather report recorded several hours earlier.

Restlessly I paced the floor, beads of perspiration popped out on my forehead. Still feeling a strange sense of smothering I opened the door that Dwaine had closed moments before. The door burst open when I touched the handle, knocking me back. Pictures were blasted off the wall and out of their frames. (Weeks later I found them behind the couch in the next room.) Dwaine strained to help me close the door and it had to be locked to keep it shut.

"Do you think we should go to the cellar?" I asked.

"I don't know. There's still no warning on the scanner, but maybe we should go to the hallway where there's some protection."

Remembering a tornado precaution, I ran to raise a window an inch in the southwest bedroom.

I looked out the window. Through the blackness I could barely see the cedar tree in our front yard. It was thrashing its branches wildly. I pressed my hot cheek against the window pane and savored the feel of cool glass. "Oh, God, protect us this night. Protect my children, too, in their little mobile home."

Rising panic subsided into a quiet peace. I marveled that this could be.

On my way back to the hall the electric power failed, but Dwaine switched on the flashlights he keeps for emergencies. "Ah! My levelheaded husband—what would I do without him!" I thought.

We began to feel pressure build in our ears. Dwaine said, "We've waited too late to go to the storm cellar. We'll have to stay put."

"Whop-a-whop-a-whop-a," it crescendoed until I thought my head or the house would explode.

Time was suspended. The house shuddered. We heard a crash. The pressure receded and was gone. Our porch and part of the roofing was blown away, but the old house stood solid.

Dwaine and I looked at each other reading each other's thoughts. "The kids! What's happened to the kids?" Our son Larry, his wife and two children lived in a mobile home at the back of our property.

As if in answer to our unspoken question, we heard someone banging on our back door. It was Larry and his family. They were frightened, wet and cold and only half dressed. We warmed them with dry blankets while they breathlessly told us what happened.

Four-year-old Brenda had awakened Larry and Jan at 11:25. She had wet her bed and needed attention. Jan had barely stripped off Brenda's clothing when Larry noticed the high wind. The trailer was rocking.

"We've got to get to Mom's cellar!" he yelled, flinging on his clothes.

Throwing a quilt around Brenda, he snatched her up and headed for the door.

"We can't. . . ." Jan started to protest.

"Now, Jan!" he insisted.

She grabbed two-year-old Brooke out of her crib and ran after Larry.

When Jan stepped out onto the porch, the wind picked her up and threw her into the side of their truck which was parked nearby. Larry ran back and pulled her toward the cellar.

The apple tree crashed behind them. Larry looked back and saw their home being blown apart.

Half of a huge pecan tree crashed in front of them, part of it across the cellar door, but Larry managed to get the door open. The wind sucked them down inside. The only injury sustained in their harrowing experience was a minor scratch to Jan's leg.

After assuring myself that my little brood suffered no physical harm, my thoughts turned to my daughter, who lives in another city. Knowing she would be terribly alarmed when she heard the news of the storm, I rushed to the phone and dialed her number. This was the only call we were able to make for several days and the miracle of it didn't register then. At that time, I didn't know all the telephone lines were down.

Dwaine and Larry left us to check on our neighbors and friends—returning occasionally to give us a report.

Our immediate neighbors were uninjured, but Mrs.

Stewart, who is elderly and partially disabled, was afraid of the dark. I found some candles and carefully climbed over the wreckage to her front porch to get them to her.

My heart ached when word came that my childhood friend, John, was among those who were killed.

The long night wore on. The wind had long since died and Dwaine used his bulldozer to clear the streets for emergency vehicles. Civil Defense joined the men of the town in their search for the dead and the injured. Women workers were brought in to sit with the elderly. A neighbor brought her child's outgrown clothing for Brenda, who had finally gotten warm wearing Grandpa's T-shirt. It had served the purpose but hadn't fit too well.

Helicopters flew over with their searchlights illuminating the area—the media had arrived.

There were no fires. The main electrical power feeder went out the moment the tornado struck, which eliminated the danger from live electrical wires. The townsmen had turned off as many of the gas meters as they could until Oklahoma Natural Gas Company could cut off the supply to the city.

When the morning dawned bright and clear, other reports filtered in.

Our close friends' daughter had run into their bedroom seconds before the windows exploded in her bedroom, embedding shards of glass in the bed and carpet. The master bedroom they were in, was the only room in the house that wasn't heavily damaged.

I had anxiously awaited word of eighty-year-old Anna, who is my mother in the Lord. Dwaine reported that she was banged up quite a bit but still on her feet. Her little house didn't have a window left in it and a wheelbarrow was lying in her living room. She managed to crawl under a desk and stay there until someone came for her. She said later, "I will never forget the darkness and the crashing sounds, but Jesus was my refuge and He kept me safe from harm."

Dwaine's sister, Laveda, and her family huddled in their hallway. Her son, who had been in the bedroom, dived for the hallway just as the tornado tore the bedrooms and the roof from their house. Laveda said, "I thought we would die, but I kept praying!"

I walked downtown. I could not believe my eyes. A knot formed in the pit of my stomach. Dwaine had not told me half. Our town was gone—only one business remained. It was a miracle anyone in town was alive!

I wandered around in a daze. When I looked northeast from Main street, there was nothing to obstruct my view to the far edge of town. It looked like a war zone and that impression was emphasized by the presence of the National Guard, who had sealed off the town to protect us from looters.

Amid the ugliness of wreckage and rubble, a beauty emerged: man's concern for his fellow man. Neighbors embraced each other; the indomitable spirit of the people picked them up from the ruins of their possessions. Their courage to rebuild came to the front.

We will ever be indebted to those who helped us in those first days—the Red Cross, the Salvation Army, the Oklahoma Southern Baptist disaster units that furnished hot food, clothing and shelter, and the Mennonite men who helped with the astronomical task of clean-up and rebuilding.

The building of United Pentecostal Church was completely destroyed. The Methodist Church opened their doors for Pentecostal services until the time the people could rebuild.

The night of miracles story is not mine alone. Each resident has his own story to tell. But, there were times in the ensuing days when I felt it was uniquely mine, especially when I learned the main force of the tornado, with its 200 m.p.h. winds, had a collision course with my house.

Two blocks away it had veered slightly to the north, causing it to miss us by one-half block. This was what spared my children. Dwaine and I in our house might have survived a direct hit, but our children could have never survived their trip to the cellar.

I learned much about trusting the Lord that night. On the verge of panic, while watching our thirty-foot cedar tree thrash about in the front yard, a mental picture of that tree crushing our house flashed through my mind. As I prayed and the peace of God descended on me, I visualized my entire family in the hollow of His hand.

We lost the cedar tree that night. It was twisted out of the ground by the roots and gently leaned against the eaves of our house. It hardly scratched the house. And the storm hardly scratched our family. A miracle? I believe so.

Aerial View: United Pentecostal Church upper left, Water Tower upper right, Renold's Lumber Co. lower right.

United Pentecostal Church.

Back of Larry and Jan's trailer, our house in background.

United Pentecostal Church Pastor's study.

Residential area.

Renolds Lumber Co. - side view.

Church and water tower behind houses.

Water tower.

CHAPTER TWO

Saved From The Fire

by LaJoyce Martin

"Run!" I screamed, as the whole room exploded.

"She's gone. She's dead," thought my mother-in-law, looking back into the boiling inferno of flames that had engulfed me. "I wish I could save her...but there's nothing I can do."

My tombstone should have read: DIED NOV. 6, 1962. I had lived twenty-five short years.

It started out like any other fall day in eastern New Mexico. Brisk, cool, invigorating. Only this day was special. It was my father-in-law's fifty-first birthday.

My husband, Elroy, and I had been married for three and a half years and were on the evangelistic field. We had stopped by Hobbs between revivals to celebrate the occasion with his folks.

Elroy took his dad to the caliche pit approximately three miles from town for target practice with the guns—to get him out of the house while we prepared the birthday dinner and wrapped the gifts.

Rachel, Elroy's younger sister, was a senior in high school, I rode with my mother-in-law to school to pick her up at dismissal time, all the way across town.

Sister Martin glanced at the kitchen range before we left to make sure no fires were left on under the food. We had purchased Brother Martin a suit and had it hanging in a plastic garment bag near the table in the combination kitchen-dining room, an annex of the L-shaped 100' x 75' beige brick church at 415 W. Scharbauer.

But alas, we had forgotten a bow for one of the birthday packages, so we made a hurried stop at a downtown store.

A bit belatedly, we dashed home to finish our preparations before the men got back. I sensed something was wrong when we drove into the yard. Running in ahead of the others, I was appalled to see hungry flames licking up from the stove, threatening to set the whole cabinet afire. Apparently, after we left to pick up Rachel, a burner with the gas turned on, had ignited.

Fumes filled the room. Supposing the blazing saucepan on the front left grate contained beans or corn, I ran to the sink and filled a large yellow glass mixing bowl with water, and hurried to the stove to put out the fire.

"DON'T...!" Sister Martin did not have time to tell me that the pan held burning grease; the water had already left the bowl. She scrambled for the back door. I had supplied the oxygen for the inflamable gasses and created a bomb!

The bowl exploded from my hands, shattering onto the floor. All I could see was angry sheets of fire everywhere—above me, below me, on all sides of me! There was no way out.

Rachel, who was near the front door, could see the flames through the window. She stumbled out into the yard in a state of shock, crying for someone to help, believing that her entire family was perishing in the fire. Sister Martin had run toward the back exit, frantically searching for a way to rescue me from certain death. I was in the middle of the kitchen, in the center room of the house.

At exactly seven minutes after four o'clock, Elroy looked at his watch. "Dad," he said, trying to keep alarm out of his voice, "we need to go home now." God had warned him that we had a fire at the house, but he did not share the premonition with his father.

Since early childhood, the name of Jesus had pulled me through every crisis, rescued me from every danger. I needed Him now; I was in a fiery furnace!

Desperately, I called out, "JESUS!"

"Why, she's still alive in that fire!" my mother-in-law thought, still frozen in the doorway at the end of the hallway.

Fire blocked my path in all directions. I could not see which way to go. I bumped into the table and the refrigerator, finding my way through the hall. The ornament hanging from the ceiling of the hall by a string, had already burned and fallen to the floor.

Poor Sister Martin! I could not see her standing in the doorway, and when I burst from the flames, I sent her sprawling. "You just shouldn't have been in God's way!" I said later.

The flash fire burned itself out quickly, leaving the sheetrock on the ceiling bubbled, the tile floor sticky, wax on a paper cup evaporated, the cotton backing on the fiberglass curtains burned, the plastic suit bag melted, and the face of the kitchen clock blackened with white behind the hands showing seven minutes after four o'clock as the time of the explosion.

I was wearing a 100% cotton pink-and-white striped seersucker dress and a synthetic headscarf. Yet, not a hair of my head was singed, nor was there any smell of smoke on my clothing. Elroy, along with his dad, came in shortly, and he sat me down on the lawn to check my eyelashes! They were still straight; the heat didn't even curl them! My only injuries were bruises where I ran into the table and the refrigerator, and two tiny spots on one foot where either hot water or grease had splattered!

The insurance adjustors came to survey the destruction. Besides the localized damage, the smoke had been sucked through the air conditioner ducts to other parts of the building.

"Weren't you people lucky that there was no one in the building when it happened," one of the men commented.

"Oh, but I was in there!" I replied. I could tell he did not believe me.

I talked to a fireman of the city later, telling him exactly what had happened. "You have no idea how many people we've pulled out of flash fires just like that—dead," he told me.

Every day that I have lived since that day in 1962 belongs to God, because He has given me a special gift of life. I owe them all to Him. One year to the day later, on November 6, 1963, He gave me my first child, Kevin, whom I dedicated to Him and His Kingdom.

The Three Hebrew Children have nothing on me! That same Jesus was in the fire with me, covering me with His asbestos suit and walking me right out to safety!

And you wonder why I love and adore Jesus?

My husband and I the year of the explosion: 1962.

Bro. & Sis. Frank Martin standing at the back exit, through which I passed to get out, the spot near where I sat on the lawn.

A front view of the church at 415 W. Scharbauer, Hobbs, New Mexico, where the explosion took place.

CHAPTER THREE

The Sparrow

by Bill Hughes

This is a true story about a little sparrow and what happened in the fall of 1961.

I was driving north from Birmingham, Alabama, for Hoover Motor Express enroute to Louisville, Kentucky.

Just south of Scottsville, Kentucky, a severe rain and wind storm developed. The clouds were heavy and black. Everybody had their lights on, although it was in the middle of the day. The asphalt highway was very slick. The rain and wind were coming from the west and blowing almost parallel to the ground. I had my windows up tight on the driver's side, but the wind was blowing rain all over me through the cracks around the door. My right window was down as the windshield was fogging up, and I needed all the air I could get on the inside of the windshield.

The tractor I was driving was a short nosed White, better known among the drivers as a "needle nose

White." The windshield and windows were small and a driver of my size had to drive with his head in a "bowing" position. The wiper blades were too short, and driving in a heavy rain, I had to bow even a little lower, with my head about ten inches from the top of the steering wheel. My hands were positioned approximately ten inches apart from the center of the top of the steering wheel.

Just as I approached the city limits of Scottsville, Kentucky, a sparrow flew in through the open window and lit between my hands facing me. He was chirping to the top of his little voice, and every time I glanced at him, he was looking me right in the eye! He was raising his wings one at a time doing a balancing act as I steered, trying desperately to keep the truck on the road. I remember speaking to the little bird and telling him to get out before he caused me to wreck.

After about ten or twelve seconds, the sparrow flew out. He left the same way he came in. I began to feel very strongly that this little sparrow was sent by God as a warning for me to stop the truck. As I pulled up to the square in Scottsville, Kentucky, I could go no further. I sat there fifteen minutes until the storm passed.

"Had God sent that little sparrow to warn me?" I asked myself.

My eyes began to search the highway as I drove on, looking for casualties of the storm. Less than a mile down the road, a small Ford Falcon had spun out of the southbound lane, going across the northbound lane, and finally coming to rest in a muddy clearing. Thank God, no one was hurt. There wasn't even a scratch on the car.

Two things I have thought of many times: (1) A bird which accidentally flies into a moving vehicle is wild! He flies all around, bumping into the glass trying desperately to get out. This sparrow did none of that. He came in, perched on the steering wheel, spoke his piece and left the same way he came. (2) How did this little sparrow fly against such a strong wind? He was flying directly into the wind, a wind that was blowing heavy rain, leaves, and small limbs almost parallel with the ground. Gusts of wind at times almost caused me to jack knife, knocking the heavy truck about like a toy, as they hit the side of the truck.

During my twenty years as a professional truck driver, I have faced what seemed like certain death many times. Each time I have found Someone else in control. I have always had a feeling that Someone was riding beside me telling me at times when to stop and when to go. Oh, I cannot see that Someone, yet I can feel His presence. It's just as strong as a gusty wind.

CHAPTER FOUR

His Wonders In The Deep

by Bill Taylor
(As told to Loren A. Yadon)

Seventy miles out in the Gulf of Mexico seemed like a strange place to meet God. I had met Him before in numerous ways, but I did not realize how quickly divine help could be summoned. Psalm 107:23-24 took on a new significance on May 13, 1984: "They that go down to the sea in ships, that do business in great waters; these see the works of the LORD, and his wonders in the deep."

The Getty Oil Company production platform, called "West Cameron 405A," off the Louisiana coast was the address where God made a rescue on that Sunday.

There were only two of us, Don Stringfellow and myself, making up the crew on the platform that serviced four natural gas wells. Most of our work involved monitoring and maintaining production equipment. On this particular evening, Don and I decided to clean some production equipment located on the second deck in preparation for an inspection that would take place the next day.

It was 9:00 p.m. and the sea was very calm. All outward evidences pointed toward a beautiful late spring evening. Little did we know what lay ahead!

Following our normal routine and procedure, we commenced to clean a gas production separator. Don heard an alarm sound in the living quarters on the top deck above us. We both decided to go upstairs and investigate the problem.

The alarm indicated that gas was escaping in the living quarters. Because we could not smell the natural gas, we opened the outside door for ventilation. This proved to be disastrous. The warm evening air caused the thermostat on the air conditioning unit to activate. Apparently the spark of electrical current on the thermostat ignited the escaping natural gas and created a tremendous explosion.

I was about ten feet ahead of Don and approaching the kitchen area of the living quarters when the explosion took place. In the lightning speed of events, my coworker was caught in the hallway where the fire was centered, and was burned to a crisp. A maze of gas explosions and balls of fire rolled down the hallway. I was literally blown against a counter ten feet away, almost knocking me unconscious. When I tried to pick myself off the floor, I saw fire dancing from all the kitchen appliances. It actually looked like hell. . .a lake of fire.

In my frantic effort to escape, I pushed open an exit door which had been jammed by the concussion. Part of the building was blown away as I surveyed the scene outside. I was not aware of any injuries at this time, but the fire had gone under my coveralls and burned my legs and arms.

In a state of shock, I instinctively ran down a small stairway leading to the main deck where we had been working that evening. As I ran across the main deck, my feet slipped from under me. Trying to catch myself, I extended my hands. I then discovered that the deck was not covered with water, but with molten fiberglass from the burning living quarters. When my hands landed in four inches of hot liquid fiberglass, the skin was literally burned off, leaving the bones and tendons exposed. The excruciating pain created a deeper state of shock.

It was almost by instinct that I ran to the other side of the platform to follow safety procedures and turn off the "Emergency Shut Down" system to prevent the whole platform from disintegrating in a major explosion similar to an atomic bomb. Any chance of survival depended on shutting down the four natural gas wells feeding that platform. In a dazed condition, with severely burned hands, and a prayer on my lips, I was able to switch off the wells.

Sitting down to gather my senses, I looked up to see the burning top deck become an arena of fire dancing like demons. A second explosion blew off the top of the living quarters which contained the helicopter pad. Floating like a parachute into the sea, it drifted away still on fire.

Fearing greater devastation, I ran to the bottom deck of the platform near the water to try to escape. Sitting down on the grating, I fell unconscious. A third explosion awoke me. I was told later that investigators found that the third explosion was the thirty ton generator building being lifted two feet off the deck. So powerful was this concussion that it seemed it was the end of the platform.

Thinking that I would rather drown than burn, I rolled off the bottom grating into the water. The safety life vest I had been wearing kept me afloat. The temperature of the water brought me to a greater awareness of what was actually happening.

When I saw that the platform was still intact, I decided to climb back on the deck and try to activate the safety capsule located on the second level. In order to do so, I had to swim against the ocean current back to the deck ladder. In my weakened condition, it must have taken thirty minutes to do so. The water seemed to seethe the burns, but when I reached the ladder, I found it terribly painful to grip the ladder rail and pull myself up. . .with hands that had very little flesh.

Once back on the lower grating, I cautiously climbed the ladder to the second deck. While walking in this inferno, I was constantly praying, calling on the name of the Lord.

Once in the eighteen men capacity capsule, I should have been able to lower the vehicle into the water. It appeared at first that the capsule may not have been intact. Part of the top deck and railing had fallen on its mechanism. To get in the capsule and attempt to lower it forty feet into the water could have risked certain death if it fell from the platform.

Without getting inside, I lowered it manually. The condition of my hands caused this effort to consume a lot of time. The safety capsule in the water dangling by a cable from the second deck presented another problem. I would have to retrace my steps across the burning deck, go down into the water and swim to the capsule.

The deck was on fire and I was afraid that the gas separation vessels would explode, completing the devastation. The steel decking above me was melting in the intense heat and dripping down on the lower deck.

Making my way through this molten rain, I did sustain some injuries as some of those metal droppings landed on my back.

More than two hours had passed since the initial explosion, and the calm seas had become choppy with a midnight wind. The suspended safety capsule bounced in the rough seas like a cork. It seemed impossible to jump back into the water and swim to the bobbing lifeboat.

The numbness of the shock had worn off and the pain became indescribable. Sitting on the bottom grating, I saw the severe condition of my hands. Asking God for strength to swim, I jumped back into the rough seas.

In spite of soggy clothes and the pain of my injuries, I felt a surge of strength that allowed me to reach the capsule. How I was able to pull myself inside the vehicle, I do not know. . .outside the divine help for which I had pled.

The safety capsule is designed to be released from the cable tying it to the platform and float on the ocean surface to allow workers to escape such incidents as this. But with my hands so badly injured, and considering the damage to the platform, I could not release the cable. Therefore the capsule remained floating in the choppy seas and tied to the fiery platform.

The wind blowing across the sea and the serious injuries combined to produce a chill that caused my body to shake violently as I lay in the bottom of the safety module. Forcing myself to kneel, I prayed that if I was to be saved from this awesome tragedy that God would send help.

For approximately eight hours, I lay in the capsule as the sea slammed it against the legs of the burning platform. I was afraid that if I was not rescued in a short time, I would either die of exposure or perish by being crushed in the craft crashing against the platform legs.

Opening a hatch on the top of the covered capsule, I fired the flare gun, which is stored on board, seven times. I was trying to signal for someone to come to my rescue. With my hands in such a terribly raw condition, I don't know how I was able to do that. If I had missed the hatch, the flare would have burned me to death.

Since the nearest platform was ten miles away, it was unlikely that anyone could see my feeble attempts calling for help. Because it was the weekend, there were not as many personnel working in the area. The chances of being rescued were less than normal.

A work boat, which serviced the various Conoco Oil Company platforms, was approximately twenty miles downstream when the crew saw the top of the living quarters afloat but still on fire. The platform's name was visible on the debris. The captain happened to know the exact location of the platform, so he immediately ordered the boat to head that direction. One hour later, while the boat was still five miles away, the crew could see the platform burning.

Because I was lying in the bottom of the safety capsule I was not discovered immediately. In a semi-conscious daze, I was barely able to pull myself to the opening and cry for help. The captain sent two men onto the platform in a brave attempt to find Don Stringfellow. His charred remains lay in the rubble.

The seas had become so rough that removing me from the capsule to the work boat was no small task. Finally, the captain had the capsule lashed to the side of the boat while I hung tenaciously to the capsule railing. It took two or three men to lift me onto the deck of the boat.

In my dazed condition, I never learned the names of these God-sent rescuers. Trained in first aid, they wrapped me in a mattress to increase my body temperature and began to feed me liquids. These initial measures probably were vital to my survival until I got to a hospital hours later.

I was transported to another platform ten miles away. After being lifted off the boat by a crane, I was immediately placed in an emergency helicopter which had been called to the scene. The hand of God was incredibly involved with my rescue!

The chopper flew directly to John Sealy Hospital in Galveston, Texas, where I was placed in the Intensive Care Unit for burn patients. The medical team was competent and compassionate. They informed me that I would have to be washed in a sterilizing vat. The process would be very painful, but the staff promised to help me.

After being placed in a strapped sling, I was hoisted into a ninety gallon tank of 80^0 water mixed with six gallons of Purex. As I washed, the pain was unbearable. Pieces of damaged flesh were pulled off my body to prevent infection.

For the next three weeks, the pain remained a constant factor as the medical staff removed my bandages every two hours and soaked me in that cleansing vat. After each washing, I would be covered with a salve containing sulphur, which would help eat the dead skin. Doses of morphine were administered to help me endure the pain.

In spite of my suffering, I became aware of the other patients, some of whom were in a worse condition than myself. The cursings and railings from their rooms caused me to pray for them and their families. My heart was burdened for them because they were cursing and accusing the same God who had been so merciful to me.

My condition was tenuous as I hung between life and death. At times I could overhear the doctors discussing certain details with my wife, Yvonne, that let me know that I might not survive. At one time, my kidneys and stomach had stopped functioning. My left leg had blood poisoning. I also contracted a staph infection which is common among burn patients.

During this life threatening period, the prayer bands at my local church, the Pentecostals of Alexandria, Louisiana, interceded on my behalf. The close support of my wife, Yvonne, my pastors, G. A. and Anthony Mangun, and a host of close friends gave me the necessary encouragement to continue to fight for my life.

During my recovery, I could not help but pray for the family of my co-worker, Don Stringfellow, during their time of grief. After being burned over 42% of my body, I wondered why I had been "snatched from the burning" instead of Don. My heart ached for them.

Skin was grafted on both my hands. If the grafts had not been successful, I would have died of the eventual infection. The doctors had spoken to Yvonne about amputating two fingers of my left hand that had been burned so severely, but she refused to allow that surgery. Eight months after the accident, I was almost 80% recovered. Three operations were performed to remove the webbing between my fingers, and I had 80% of my normal grip. . . in the left hand which doctors had said I might never use again.

Amazed at my rapid recovery, the doctors have used me as an example to other patients of the miracle of recovery. I give credit not only to the doctors and medical staff but to God. I believe that I am a walking testimony to the power of prayer. To have survived the blast, endured the exposure of the seas with severe burns, and conquered the infection in the hospital is not one, but many miracles.

It is strange how an incident of this nature can change a person's perspective. During this ordeal, I realized what really constituted important values in life. The God who heard me as a badly burned man on the lower deck of the burning platform gives me the peace to go through a career change. I now want to devote the rest of my life to helping people in need because I know the mercy of God escorted me from hell itself.

It would be wonderful for us to meet personally and shake hands. Just that friendly gesture in itself would confirm the wonders of God in the deep.

Production platform before explosion.

Platform after explosion with safety capsule seen in water at lower right.

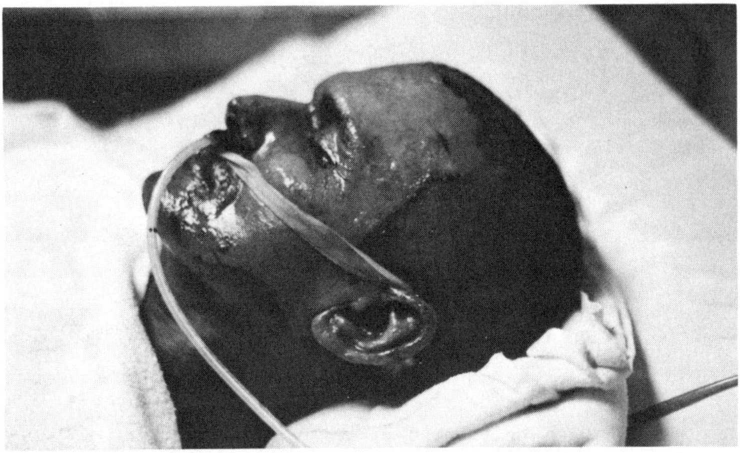

Bill Taylor at John Sealy Hospital Burn Center, Galveston, Texas fighting for his life.

Bill (left) shows Loren his hands as he tells him his story of deliverance.

CHAPTER FIVE

Trapped In The Fire

by Angelea Whisler

Editor's Note: *All mankind shares similar experiences. Each life has its triumphs and also its tragedies. The Christian, however, rests in the assurance that "The steps of a good man are ordered of the LORD" (Psalm 37:23). He also believes that "All things work together for good to them that love God" (Romans 8:28). When danger, destruction and death come, the Christian looks for the hand of God in the event. If he escapes (as Angelea Whisler did in the following story), he gives thanks and recognizes God in the deliverance. The sinner, on the other hand, might say, "I lucked out" or "It wasn't my time to go."*

When the Christian seems to be defeated by suffering and death, he says, "The LORD gave, and the LORD hath taken away; blessed be the name of the LORD" (Job 1:21) and he finds comfort even in pain and grief. The sinner, however, asks, "Why?" and rails at fate and the unknown fear and despair.

This story is included in this book not because it reveals the miraculous intervention of God but because it illustrates the proper attitude of a Christian toward crisis situations. Since the author is a Christian, she sees God working in the crisis to save her life, and she gives thanks to Him. This is proper. But the story does not ignore that "good and bad" happen to every person whether he is a Christian or not. Many sinners have been delivered through similar experiences, but he often fails to give credit to God.

This true story should help us accept whatever happens in life as being under the canopy of God's knowledge and grace.

The past few years had been a busy, tiring time for me tending to my family's needs both spiritually and materially. But all three of our children had finished school. Lori, our daughter, had married and both of our sons, Stephen and Mark, were employed and no longer dependent on us. It seemed to be the opportune time to take that long-needed vacation.

As King David longed for a drink of water from the wells of Bethlehem, I had a strong desire to visit "The garden of Eden" of my childhood in the springtime. I was born and spent the first thirteen years of my life on a farm in the rolling hills of southeastern Oklahoma, in the community of Ringold. It was thirty-eight years since my family moved to California. I had returned several times to visit, but none of these visits were in the springtime. I remembered the beauty of the springtime with the dogwoods and redbuds in bloom and the meadows filled with daisies, buttercups and pansies, and listening to the rippling brooks. This also was the place where as a child, I had received the Holy Ghost and was baptized in Jesus' name.

Glen, my husband, was unable to take a vacation at the time due to the springtime planting on the farm. My mother and her seventy-three year old friend wanted to go to Oklahoma. I drove the three of us. The other lady went to her daughter who lived near Henryetta.

My mother and I went on to Skiatook to visit my sister, Oleta Biggs. After visiting a few days with her, we drove to Antlers, Oklahoma, which is approximately twenty-five miles from Ringold, to visit my aunt, who lived five miles east of Antlers on highway 7. We spent Saturday night with her and attended Sunday school the next morning. That afternoon we went to Ringold to visit with friends and see the beauty of the countryside. The dogwoods and redbuds were in full bloom.

Back in Bakersfield, California, my daughter had attempted to telephone that Sunday afternoon while I was out. She left a message that she would telephone again that evening, so at 11:30 p.m. (Oklahoma time) she called. We had a long visit before I went to bed about midnight.

Glen, Stephen and Mark had been in a good service that day at the Pentecostal Lighthouse in Visalia, California. After church they had gone out with friends for refreshments and a time of fellowship. It was about 11:00 o'clock before they got home (1:00 a.m. Oklahoma time).

At 1:30 a.m. two loud noises like an explosion awoke me from a sound sleep. I jumped out of bed, astonished as I saw the wall of the bedroom and bathroom collapse to the floor completely engulfed in flames. My first thoughts and concern was to get my eighty-year-old mother out of the house. I got her by the arm and led her out the back door to safety.

My uncle was trying to control the fire. As I led my mother out, I kept hearing my uncle say, "Call the fire department!" On my way out with my mother, I passed the telephone. After helping her out the door, I walked back to the telephone, approximately twenty feet from the door, to call the fire department. By the time I finished the call, the back of the house was filled with smoke and engulfed in flames.

Earlier that evening I had observed my aunt open the front door, so I thought I would go out the front door since the fire had not reached that area.

When I reached the front door, however, it had a chain latch. I unfastened it and attempted to open the door, but it would not move. Unknown to me the door had a dead bolt lock which opened with a key. Looking at the back door, I said to myself, "I don't think I can make it through all the fire and smoke. If I don't make it, they will never find me in the fire, so I had better stay near this front door."

By nature I am a person easily excited, but after I could not open the door I calmly said to myself, "Well, is this my time?" The thought of leaving my husband and children entered my mind. I knew it was in God's hands. But like the time Jesus said "Peace be still" to the winds and waves, a great calmness came over me.

When I was only four years old, my parents received the Holy Ghost. From their life and teaching faith was instilled into my heart. We relied on prayer for healing.

When I was a small child, I was healed of an earache, and this was the beginning of my faith in God that continued to grow through the years. Now trapped in the fire, my faith was needed more than ever.

After I could not open the door, I noticed the drapes over the front window. After I pulled the drapes to see if it was a possible way of escape, I felt around to find something to break the glass window. As I lay on the floor feeling around, I drifted into unconsciousness. That was another one of God's ways of protecting me. I later learned that the window had iron bars over it and I would not have been able to get out even if I had broken the window. Moreover, the broken window would have caused the flames to be immediately pulled to where I was.

My mother told the men that I was in the house. My uncle and two men began trying to break down the door to rescue me. Their efforts were not successful. But one of the men who was an Indian said, "I am going to give it one more try." He backed a distance from the door, ran and threw his weight against the door. This time the door broke open, but immediately the flames leaped out the opening. But I was lying unconscious at the door.

The Indian and my uncle were able to pull me out and into the bed of a pickup truck. My mother and aunt prayed as they worked to revive me. My mind was thinking, "Oh! I am so peaceful and resting so good! Why don't they let me sleep!"

They rubbed my burned arms, which caused the first pain I felt. I heard my mother's voice calling my name. "If you hear me say something, Angelea."

I thought I answered her, but they said I just took a deep breath. I drifted back into unconsciousness. An ambulance arrived and the attendant gave me oxygen. I was taken to a little hospital in Antlers.

My family in California was given the news of the tragedy. Glen and Lori were on the first flight leaving for Dallas, Texas. They were met at the airport and arrived in Antlers about 4 p.m. Glen began to make arrangements to transfer me to the burn center at Hillcrest Memorial Hospital in Tulsa. I arrived, by ambulance, at Hillcrest at 1:00 a.m. that morning. First they attempted to transport me by helicopter but due to a storm it was only able to get as far as McAlester then had to return to Tulsa.

I spent ten days in the intensive care unit but after spending almost a month in the hospital the day finally arrived when I was able to be released to return home in California.

When Glen received the news of my accident, he called our pastor, Brother James McPhaill, and our church family begin to pray. Many other friends also prayed and I continued to improve. When I was released from the hospital, I was unable to speak in an audible voice. A few days later some of the church people visited me and when they started to leave they prayed for me. I raised my hands to praise God and as I was praying the words, "Thank You, Jesus" came from my lips. From that day I knew I would talk once again. In a few weeks I was able to talk more clearly. About six months later I had minor surgery to remove polyps from my vocal cords, that was possibly caused from blisters on my vocal cords due to the intensity of the heat and the length of time I was in the house. This has been the only problem I have encountered due to the fire.

The fire department determined the cause of the fire was that lightning had struck the house two days prior to our arrival but they thought it had only struck their hot water heater which was in the bathroom. However, the fire had entered into the insulation of the house and had been smoldering in it for two days. That night when we went to bed my aunt had turned on the attic fan which began to fan the smoldering insulation causing it to ignite into flames.

I think that it was a miracle of God that my life was spared.

CHAPTER SIX

My Shield of Faith

by Shirley Welch

Have you ever heard of a tragic happening and in your subconscious mind begin to think, "Other people! Those things happen to other people?"

Well, much to my surprise and dismay in October 1975, I became one of the "other people."

We were at our annual Junior Class Sunday School party where we played games, bobbed for apples, and roasted weiners by the campfire. As the fun-filled evening came to an end, my husband and I climbed into the car, very tired from our busy schedule of the day, much too tired and unprepared to face the situation which we encountered as we walked into our home.

The house was too quiet. As the late afternoon sunshine spilled into the living room, it broke into a patchwork pattern on the gold carpet. We had expected our teenage daughter, Beverly, to welcome us at the door, but all that greeted us was dead silence. I went to her room thinking she might be resting. Instead, there I was, faced with one of those situations that always happens to "other people."

I saw the note stating that she had "ran away from home," and beside it were the tresses of her beautiful, long brown hair.

The questions began to swirl in my mind. "Where is she? Who is she with? How long has she been gone? Is she safe? This can't be! I'm dreaming! No, God! Not my child! I can't stand not knowing if she's all right! There is so much evil in this world. No, God! Don't let harm come to her."

We cried and prayed as hours passed, hours that seemed like eternity. Each time the phone rang we frantically answered hoping to hear her voice. No one knew what we were experiencing, and as we received our regular calls, we tried to remain calm and nonchalant, hoping the conversation would end quickly so the line would be clear for her call. Night was fast coming. "Please God, let me hear from her before dark. Please. . . ."

> *"I love the LORD, because he hath heard my voice and my supplications. Because he hath inclined his ear unto me, therefore will I call upon him as long as I live" (Psalm 116:1-2).*

Finally, the call came. She had spent hours at a shopping mall in a beauty shop trying to repair the "chopped job" she had done when she cut her hair.

This was the beautiful little girl that I gave to God as a baby and "trained in the way she should go." I saw her baptized in Jesus' name at an early age and filled with the Holy Ghost, never missing a church service, involved in all the activities of the church. But when the cancer of worldliness began eating at her spirit, I was not even aware of it. As I looked at her, it was not her hair that was my greatest concern, but in her eyes I saw an evil spirit glaring back at me—rebellion! The hair would grow out, but now it was my time to do battle with this ugly, strong-willed spirit.

> *"For we wrestle not against flesh and blood, but against principalities, against powers, against the rulers of the darkness of this world, against spiritual wickedness in high places" (Ephesians 6:12).*

I prepared for battle. "Am I dressed properly?" I asked myself. Truth, righteousness, preparation of the gospel of peace, helmet of salvation, sword of the spirit. But something is missing—my shield of faith. Frantically I searched my heart for it, but I could not find it. But I had to have it to win this most important battle with Satan.

The next week was a busy one because we were having a city-wide crusade reaching for souls. Satan was there, also, with his slurs and snares. "Reach a city? You can't even reach your own daughter!"

After much prayer and many tears, there seemed to be no change in Beverly's attitude. Each day she was more withdrawn and stronger willed. Rebellion really had its ugly fingers clinched with a death grip.

As the first service of the crusade began on Wednesday night in the city auditorium, the crowds came and we sang and worshiped and praised God. There she was a girl who had once danced in the spirit and worshiped God—so different now. She stood with face drawn, arms folded, mouth clenched in defiance.

As Thursday and Friday nights came, I thought, "Surely it will happen tonight. God, save my girl. Don't let her be lost." I kept hoping for change, but I still had not located my lost piece of armor—my shield of faith.

If it did not happen Wednesday, Thursday or Friday, then it had to be Saturday because that was the last night of the crusade. The ex-hippies all told everyone there that the world had nothing to offer but loneliness, emptiness, and pain. Surely she would listen to them because they had come out of a world that she was looking at with such longing. Saturday night service came to a close and, much to my disappointment, my daughter had not changed or seemingly been touched.

I went home bone-weary, tired and disappointed. For weeks we had worked so hard sending out announcements, special choir practices, and all the things it takes to produce a big crusade. I collapsed into bed about midnight. At 2:00 a. m. I was awakened by the presence of God and a still small voice whispering in my ear. "If you will get up and go pray for Beverly, I will answer your prayer."

Tired and weary as I was, I somehow received strength to get up and walk to her room. As I walked into her room, I found it—*my shield of faith*—glistening in the moonlight. I hugged it tightly to my chest and walked over to her bed. Stretching my hand over her head, I said, "In Jesus' name, it is done."

She did not awaken, but there arose such faith in my soul as I had never experienced before. A wheel of joy flipped over in my soul and replaced the heaviness. I was so excited that I could barely wait until morning. Peacefully, I went back to bed and slept soundly until morning.

As the first particles of sunlight filtered through the curtains, doubt and heaviness began to attack me, but I remembered the words of the Lord. "If you will get up and go pray for Beverly I will answer your prayer." "I will!" And faith took over once again. With renewed confidence I said aloud, "I rebuke you, Satan, in Jesus' name. God has given me this day and you will not take it from me!"

And the wheel of joy turned. There was a song in my heart as I prepared for Sunday school. Faith was in action. As far as I was concerned, it had already happened. Satan had lost the battle and was on the run. The shield of faith gave me power to quench all the fiery darts of the wicked and it will do the same for anyone.

When I saw Beverly that morning, there seemed to be no change at all as I looked on her "outer man." The rebellion seemed to be making a final stab, fighting like a wounded animal. But that did not bother me, because in my heart all I could sing was, "It is finished. The battle is over. It is finished; there will be no more war. It is finished, the end of the conflict. It is finished, and Jesus is Lord!"

As church progressed that Sunday morning, my joy was more than I could contain. His Spirit came over me, and I danced before the Lord with all my might. It was my victory march!

Had Beverly changed? No, not to those who only looked on her "outer man" and saw her sullen, defiant personage. But I saw her through the eyes of faith as a radiant, submissive child of God.

Sunday afternoon passed by and in prayer I said, "Lord, I don't care how You do it but I make this one request. Let Beverly surrender of her own free will." I had decided that I did not want anyone to beg her to come to the altar.

I thank God for a church that stood behind us during this time, praying, reaching, helping, encouraging us, sharing our pain. And it also shared our victory as Beverly came to the altar that Sunday night and totally surrendered her life to God. The girl God gave back to us that night was much more full of His Spirit than she had ever been. Now she was changed completely, an example of His miracle-working power. On the following Wednesday night as the altar service was given for those who had a need, Beverly was in the line. When Papaw Welch prayed, victory came completely!

Certainly, rebellion attacked again but it never completely possessed. And as she would do battle with Satan in the future, Beverly was never too proud to reach for help, asking for prayer.

Years later I took great pride as a mother when I watched her walk down the aisle to become Mrs. Curtis Parker. It was a beautiful wedding, white lace, candles, songs, and promises. I watched their car drive off into their happy-ever-after life, not knowing that only three months later, tragedy would make its mark on their lives.

It was on Thanksgiving Day, during an early morning hunting trip. A gun accidentally discharged, and Curtis was shot in the leg below the knee. When I should have been strong and encouraging her, it was Beverly who had the faith, the song in her heart, and the trust as she would daily say, "Mother, everything is going to be all right." The smile on her face gave me courage to make it. Two weeks later after much mental anguish, the leg was amputated.

When my children returned to church a month later, they were called on to address the congregation. I shall never forget the praise she offered. "I thank God for trusting me through this trial!"

"Many daughters have done virtuously, but thou excellest them all" (Proverbs 31:29).

CHAPTER SEVEN

The Great Depression of 1983

by Judy Segraves

Yes, there was a great depression in 1929. But I went through one in 1983. And it took a miracle of God to bring me out.

I have always been a happy sort of person. My life has been full of blessings. For nineteen years I have been married to a minister, and we have two charming children.

Some time ago, I faced a series of inner struggles, and a war began. The foe was wicked in the combat, but my weapons were not of this world.

With the help of my husband and a strong desire to win, I am now free. Free to tell you that no obstacle is too big if you want to be an overcomer.

When I became a victim of depression, oppression, and fear, my heart and mind and body were all affected. I was a miserable mess.

My husband was asked to serve as an executive vice president of one of our Bible colleges in Stockton, California. He was excited about the move, but I was apprehensive. The promotion was something to be proud of, but I did not want to leave my friends or the area. It was my home.

Leaving the pastorate meant I would be leaving my post also. "I don't know if I will fit into this new role. It will be so different from that of a pastor's wife." I reminded my husband Dan of my apprehensions on many occasions.

"Of course, you will," he would respond. "You are perfect for anything. You'll like it after you get there." He encouraged me daily.

It just so happened that there was a vacancy for a worker in the college cafeteria. My mother seemed a likely candidate for the job, and we made arrangements for her to move the two thousand miles with us.

She was happy about the move. We arrived in Stockton in late August. Five days later I walked into her bedroom to find her dead. At the age of fifty-three, she had suffered a heart attack. The shock and resulting trauma I suffered inside were almost more than I could handle. Outwardly I appeared calm and controlled. Inside, something ugly grew.

California was so different from my home. People of all races melted into the city. I walked into my son's room one day to see a dark skinned Indian walk by the window, his head wrapped in a turban. I feared these people of different cultures. "What are they really like?" I asked.

The constant fear and depression triggered mental and physical sickness.

"Dan, did you hear that?" Trembling I raised up in bed.

"What? Hear what?"

"I don't know. Please check the house!"

He pulled himself sleepily out of bed to go investigate.

Clammy fingers seemed to grasp for my shaking body.

"I'm sorry," I apologized. "I know you have to teach first hour tomorrow. But will you just hold me? I don't know what is wrong."

Though I felt guilty waking him, it gave me comfort to know he was close. Many nights I did not wake him, but would tip-toe through the house looking for what I knew was not there. I remembered that the Bible said that we have guardian angels about us, so I would try to picture an angel standing at each corner of our house with its sword of protection extended.

My body began to react to the mental sufferings, and I became physically ill. When night would come, suffocating fears pressed upon me. The weight I carried would not lift.

Each month when an inspirational magazine we subscribed to arrived, I read of the battles fought and won by others. Hope would spring up again, but it lasted for only a time. Depression then crept back.

Through the years I have been saturated with the knowledge that unlimited possibilities lie within. I have read the Bible through each year for almost a decade. I know its promises and that all things are possible through God.

My husband is a possibility thinker. He obtained a cassette tape that spoke about the power of imaging or visualizing what you want to happen. Actually this is simple faith. I listened to it several times. It seemed so easy. I often thought about this principle.

But my spirit and body were depleted. Why should a blessed woman be in such a state? One day I simply tired of it. I knew there had to be a way to overcome. And I set out to do it!

Knowing the battle would be fierce, I set my mind for the fight and began to gather the weapons I needed. I wanted to be again happy, joyful, smiling.

I examined myself. Since a small child, God had been first. He still was. I knew in my heart that I loved him still. He was my closest Friend.

I realized I needed the support of others. I went to church regularly to gain strength from fellowship and to renew my mind in worship and praise.

I talked to God in prayer. This was a tremendous source of strength. And I knew He understood.

I read His Word. I knew if the words of the Bible could penetrate my mind, it would also be a cleansing for my heart.

I spoke His promises aloud. I found parts of Scripture to match my feelings, and vocalized them repeatedly. His Word really is alive and true.

I occupied my mind with something constructive. I took a creative writing class at the college where my husband is an instructor. The stories and articles I wrote proved a great therapy.

I began to thank God before I saw results. I was depressed and fearful. I was still troubled physically. But I began to thank God in faith that it was leaving. I thanked Him often.

I used imaging or visualization. This was seeing myself as I wanted to be. I wanted to be happy and vibrant again. I saw myself laughing and joyous, talking to others, offering encouraging words to them, building them up.

I carried this picture within. I saw myself different. One day I realized with a start that something had happened. I *was* different. The oppression had lifted. I wanted to laugh. I wanted to cry. But this time the tears were from joy.

I have good news for those who are grappling with depression. When they feel they have reached the bottom, they can look up! It is true! Anyone can overcome if he is determined to. I know. I was down there, too.

Rev. and Mrs. Dan Segraves and family.

CHAPTER EIGHT

He Heals Headaches

by Ilene K. Dewar

On August 4, 1973, my friends Brother Bob and Sister Esther Arnold and I were part of a group of volunteers who were in Bedford, Indiana, to invite people to revival services at Christ Temple. At that time Brother Glenn Craig was pastor of the church and Sister Louise Potter from Martinsville, Indiana, was the evangelist.

On that very warm, humid Saturday afternoon, Sister Arnold and I were partners. We were assigned an area near the church because we both lived in Bloomington and were unfamiliar with Bedford.

We enjoyed this type of house-to-house evangelism; we were excited and expected to have a wonderful time. However, shortly after we began working in our area, Sister Arnold became ill. She complained of a headache, dizziness and nausea. Since we were accustomed to witnessing in all kinds of weather and under various circumstances, we decided to continue knocking on doors.

But Sister Arnold became sicker the farther we walked.

When it became evident that she could not continue, we decided to turn back in the direction of the church. We stopped at a laundromat on our way back so that she could rest. While we were there, a Pentecostal couple from the area introduced themselves to us. They told us of a great need for healing that their child had and asked for our prayers. We assured them that we would pray.

We continued to the church and were thankful that Brother Craig had left it unlocked. We hurried inside. The severity of the headache now caused Sister Arnold to hold her head and moan and groan—not her usual behavior when she is sick. She does her best to keep her pain hidden. I knew something was very wrong.

We were in a strange city with no means of transportation and no access to a telephone to call for help. The church members, Brother Craig, and Brother Arnold would probably be gone for at least another hour.

Sister Arnold lay down on the church pew near the front of the sanctuary. She asked me to pray for her. I laid hands on her head and asked the Lord to give her a healing touch. Then I walked toward the back of the sanctuary still praying silently for her. The pain continued.

"You'll have to do it again, Ilene. Pray again," she insisted.

After I laid hands on her and prayed again, I turned toward the altar to ask the Lord what I should do. Just as I turned, however, Sister Arnold very quietly and very calmly said, "The pain is gone."

For the next forty-five minutes Sister Arnold and I had a glorious praise and thanksgiving service. It was wonderful! We rejoiced in her miraculous healing. But the glory of God that came upon us in our praise was also a miracle.

Years later, Sister Arnold experienced that same kind of severe headache. When the pain became intense, she went to a hospital in St. Petersburg, Florida. The doctor who examined her suggested that she see a neurologist or neurosurgeon. When she declined to do so, the doctor gave her a pain shot, causing her to sleep for several hours. When she awoke, the headache was gone.

A few months after that episode, Sister Arnold and her husband attended special services in Springville, Indiana. During one service, the special speaker pointed to her and said that the Lord wanted to heal her of several nerves twisted in the back of her neck. That completed the healing. The headaches have not reoccurred.

CHAPTER NINE

Stress Relief

by Ruth Ann Kerr

The "whys" of my affliction are really not that important. What is important is that because of stress (and unbelief), I began to have hives in early 1980.

At first, the hives appeared a few times each week. Medication was taken to control the outbreaks. But over a very short period of time, the outbreaks were almost continual and required around-the-clock dosages of antihistamines just to enable me to function in daily activities.

In 1982 I began to suffer with anxiety attacks. For those who have never had such an attack, one is literally in a state of panic, sheer terror, and frightening palpitations of the heart. . .and for no obvious reason. These attacks are sudden and nearly always incapacitating for a short time. These anxiety attacks gradually began to accompany the outbreak of hives.

For three and one-half years I refilled prescriptions of that medication, never leaving home without an adequate supply, and always hoping that the medication would finally rid me of these reactions. I wanted deliverance but did not pray for it; I felt stress (and its related illnesses) were all "part of the territory" of a career and active church life.

But on June 11, 1984, as I sat in my office, it suddenly occurred to me that I had not had hives or an anxiety attack in five days! God had been trying to build faith in my heart for several months to believe Him, not just for others, but for the things I wanted most in my life. While I still could not voice my request for deliverance, the Lord kindly answered the cry of my soul and healed me.

Yes, I still have stress, and in some areas of my life, more than ever before. But it has been more than six months since I took any medication for hives and anxiety attacks—there has been absolutely no reoccurrence.

I thank God that we are not obligated to "just live with" afflictions and illnesses. We can go to Him, believing, and watch Him deliver us and make us whole!

CHAPTER TEN

Truth Will Stand

by Lester R. Thompson

In biblical history we read where God has oftimes performed various types of miracles to thwart harm that was intended for one or several of His people. On the other hand, when God allowed persecution and even death to come to some of His people, it was for the purpose of a greater lesson to be learned and a greater revelation to be brought to light. We are, however, asked to accept God's promises for protection. We should affirm with Solomon that "Every word of God is pure: he is a shield unto them that put their trust in him" (Proverbs 30:5).

It is with heart-felt thanks that I write the following testimonial where protection from harm was furnished me by a miracle of God.

I was conducting revival services in the little town of West Jefferson, Ohio, during the Second World War in the forties. God was blessing and adding to the church. In many cases, however, where God is blessing, the devil threatens. Such was the case in the Saturday night service. A lady, who was wellknown in the town and who had been bedridden for many months, was carried into the church to attend service. About six inches of her spine had deteriorated, making it impossible for her to walk.

During the course of the message I stressed the great importance of being saved in view of the coming of the Lord and against the day of judgment. "In fact," I said, "being saved is more important than being in good health, possessing houses and lands, having an abundance of wealth and *even the ending of wars."*

In the service there was a woman who misunderstood my fervency and the point of my message. She left the service immediately, feeling that I was very unpatriotic and was unconcerned about our fighting men on the battlefield.

The woman in question went to town, which happened to be filled with shoppers, and stirred up about twenty-five men on the basis of what I was preaching and, I am sure, some things I was *not* preaching. The men were so aroused that they came and stood outside the church, lined on both sides of the walk. According to a report the pastor received, "They came to get me."

In the meantime, however, God was preparing the way of protection by performing a miracle. When the men arrived and looked through the door, they saw the sick woman lowered into the watery grave of baptism. They also saw her come up out of the water praising God and stand upon her feet. A few minutes later they saw her walking erect back and forth in front of the altar.

The men, having seen this miracle, were amazed. When the lady walked toward the door to return to her home on her own, the men, one by one, left the premises. By the time the pastor and I left the church, there were none left to accuse or to harm.

Upon reflection of this incident, I can readily say that I believe the miracle that was performed was of three-fold value: the woman could walk again having come to the Lord; there was no harm done to me; and there were about twenty-five angry men who were persuaded that the God we serve is a God of miracles. It once more proved that a person cannot do anything *against* the truth, only for the truth. Greater is He that is in us than he that is in the world.

CHAPTER ELEVEN

He Knew Where I Was!

by Fred E. Kinzie

Recently while kneeling in prayer at one of our Saturday evening church prayer meetings, a thought, which I believe was from the Lord, crossed my mind. It was this: "Answers to our prayers come in direct proportion to the intensity of desire with which they are prayed!"

Several scriptural incidents flashed through my mind that confirmed the thought: the woman with the issue of blood; the blind man who cried out in desperation knowing that Jesus was passing by; the Apostle Paul when he turned and rebuked the devil out of the possessed girl in Phillipi; and a host of others.

Incidents of answered prayer throughout my life started coursing through my mind—and there were many of them that the prayer was answered before the words were cold on my lips. One recent incident illustrates this clearly.

It had been a long, tiresome day as Sister Kinzie and

I began walking up the west concourse of the St. Louis airport. Our journey had started that day in Salem, Oregon, traveling by automobile to Portland. Early in the afternoon we boarded a plane for Atlanta, Georgia, and after an hour's layover there, flew back to St. Louis. As we walked up the concourse, I noted the time, 11:22 p.m.

The plane had parked at the extreme west end of the concourse. It could not have parked any farther away from the luggage carousel than it was. As we were walking, loaded down with our carry-on luggage, I remarked to Sister Kinzie that the concourse looked long and I was very tired and weary! Upon reaching the baggage carousel, we waited about fifteen minutes for our luggage to arrive.

Getting it all together, we started walking toward a taxi stand when Sister Kinzie turned to me and asked, "Fred, where's your briefcase?"

"Oh, no!" I answered, lifting my hand to my forehead. "I've left it back in the plane. I set it down by my seat next to the window. Our tickets are in it and things I need for our Foreign Missions Board meeting tomorrow. I've got to go get it!"

Pulling all the luggage back near a seat, I told Sister Kinzie to wait for me as I went back to the plane, hoping the ramp door would not yet be locked.

As I walked back that long concourse it seemed my feet weighed a ton. By the time I got back to the ramp door, it was closed—and locked! Several people were lying around on the seats and floor trying to get in a few winks while waiting on their planes, which I learned later, would not be leaving until early the next morning.

I asked if anyone knew where the man was who took

care of the area, but no one seemed to have seen him lock the ramp door. The only thing I knew to do was go back to the baggage area and see if I could find someone there. So I started on that long walk again—which this time seemed twice as long. It was now 12:15 a.m.

Arriving back at the baggage carousel, I found no one around. The place looked deserted. Sister Kinzie was there alone. She asked, "Fred, did you get it?"

When I answered "No!" she asked what I was going to do.

"I don't know, but I must find a porter. Maybe he'll know who to get in touch with," I answered.

I was so tired after three trips up and down that concourse that I sat down to rest for a moment. As I sat there a porter came by to help someone else who had arrived on the same plane as we did. I got to him right away.

He told me where to find the luggage claim area for Eastern Airlines. I went but could find no one there. I reported back to the porter and he said as soon as he took care of his customer, he'd see what he could do.

Shortly thereafter, he came and said we'd go back to the plane. For the fourth time I started walking that long trip to the far end of the concourse. Upon arriving he discovered the ramp door locked and he could find no one in the vicinity that had a key. He stopped at a phone and tried to call the baggage claim area but no one answered there.

When he got no answer, I asked, "What will I do now?"

"The only thing I can tell you is to go back to the baggage area and wait until someone arrives at the claim office. I just hope they haven't gone home!" he answered.

He left, and I faced that long concourse for the fifth time. I was about two-thirds of the way back when I remembered that probably the best thing I could do was to pray.

I looked up and down that deserted concourse and not one person was in sight. As I went dragging along, I closed my eyes and prayed desperately, "Lord, you know the predicament that we're in. Please Lord, put me in touch with the right man to take care of this problem of ours. Thank you, Jesus, for the privilege of prayer!" It couldn't have taken over ten seconds to pray that prayer.

When I opened my eyes, to my amazement, walking to my left about a step in front of me was a man with an Eastern Airlines emblem on his coat sleeve. Taking a quick step, I touched his shoulder. As he turned, I asked, "Are you an Eastern employee?"

"Yes," he answered, "Why?"

"Are you the man who takes care of incoming planes?" I asked.

"Yes, I am," he answered. "Do you need something?"

I told him we had just arrived an hour ago on a plane from Atlanta and I had left my briefcase on it. It was very important that I have it as my plane tickets and other needed materials were in it.

"Why, I went through that plane not over a half-hour ago and I didn't see any briefcase. Are you sure you left it on the plane?" he questioned me.

"Yes," I answered, "I know I left it on the plane. You'd never see it if you weren't looking for it. It was leaning against the side of the plane next to the window in aisle twenty-one."

"Well, come on and we'll go back and see," he said.

So for the sixth time I started down that longer-than-ever concourse, this time, though tired out, with high hopes in my heart and a great big "Thank You, Jesus" on my lips!

When Sister Kinzie saw me coming with the brief-case, she gave a great big sigh of relief. When I told her the story of the Eastern employee, she along with me, gave a great big "Thank You, Jesus!" to the Lord!

I'll never know where that man came from. But there's one thing I'm sure of: God had him to step out beside me at the precise moment that I desperately needed him! Don't tell me God doesn't know where we are! He's only a prayer away!

Rev. and Mrs. Fred Kinzie

CHAPTER TWELVE

The Check That Blew Away

by Walter Marrs as told to Mary H. Wallace

It was payday and I had gotten my check.

"Hurry up, honey, and we'll go to the bank. Then we can do a little shopping," I called to my wife as I came in from work. We were living in West Texas at that time, and a severe sandstorm had just blown in that morning.

"Is it very windy out?" my wife quizzed me as she tied a scarf around her beautiful, gray hair.

"About fifty miles an hour according to the radio. We won't stay out in it long. We'll just use the drive-in window at the bank and then get a few groceries. And I do have to pay that house payment." I sat down at the kitchen table, made out the deposit slip, and signed my check so that everything would be ready when we got to the bank.

The sand-laden wind was still blowing hard as I wheeled into the drive-in window of the bank. I quickly rolled down the window, pulled out the teller's service drawer and laid the deposit slip with the attached check in the drawer. Swish! That wind scooped up the deposit slip and the check before the teller could pull the drawer in.

I jumped out of the car and ran after my check.

"There's something there—right in front of the bank," my wife called out.

I rushed to the front of the bank as my wife had directed, but all I found was the deposit slip. The check was no longer with it. In my search for the lost check, I happened to glance across the street. "What is that piece of paper hanging on that three inch pipe around the parking lot?" I wondered. I was tempted to dash across the street in spite of the heavy traffic, but I waited until the traffic cleared. As I hurried across the street, I kept my eyes on the piece of paper. "It is my check!" I cried excitedly, but just as I was about two steps from the check, a sudden whirlwind picked it up and carried it over the top of the store building and out of sight.

I raced down the alley behind the stores, but all I found were tumbleweeds, pieces of waste paper in all sizes and shapes, cardboard boxes, and other trash blown in by the hard wind. Despondently, I started back to the car, but when I got back to the first building, I stopped and took a final look at the top of the building. I needed that check, and since I had already signed it, I would not be able to have it replaced by my employer. I knew nothing else to do but pray. So standing in the parking lot, I lifted my voice and submitted my request to my Lord.

"Jesus, You know how I need that money. That check is already signed; anyone who finds it can cash it. Lord, You know I have to pay my tithes; then there is the house

payment that is due. Besides that we are about out of groceries. Please, Lord, let me find my check."

Just as I stopped praying, to my delight that check came floating off the top of that building, floating over the side toward me. I immediately gave thanks to the Lord, and then I realized a most incredible and unbelievable thing; the check was floating *crosswise to the wind's direction!* Completely amazed, I stood watching the check continue its flight contrary to the wind for fifteen or twenty feet.

Slowly the check settled and came to rest on the ground. I took one step and picked it up. I had to give thanks to God for this miracle He so graciously performed just for me.

"Thank You, Jesus, for giving it back to me. I know that only You could have done this. You do still control the winds."

(Editor's Note: Brother Walter Marrs, Henderson, Texas shared this story with me and it was first published in the WAP Adult Take-home paper, "The Vision." Used by permission.)

CHAPTER THIRTEEN

God Answers Prayer—Even For Small Things

by A. W. Post

During the Depression, Dick Stanley and I were roommates at Bible school. Times were tough and occasionally we did not have money to buy food.

I recall one instance when Dick and I were alone in our room, and feeling quite hungry. We knelt in prayer and quietly asked the Lord to give us a chow mein sandwich, which at that time was quite a bountiful sandwich. About ten minutes later a student (who had never treated us before and never treated us afterward) came into our room and invited Dick and me to the restaurant down the street from the school. He said, "I will buy you each a chow mein sandwich." We were blessed over that more than if he had bought us a steak dinner, because that was exactly what we had asked the Lord for.

In the early days of my ministry, we were in home missions work, opening up a new church with the help of Howard and Mary Reed. I had a pressing need and prayed for the Lord to send me $12.00 in the mail the next morning. I was upstairs studying when the mail came, so Howard got the mail. I called down to Howard and asked him if there was any mail for me. He answered, "No."

I refused to let unbelief get into my heart, so I went on reading. Shortly afterwards Howard came upstairs and informed me that two weeks before they had taken an offering for me in the church where his mother was the secretary-treasurer. She had been busy and had not had time to send the offering to me, so she sent the check in his letter. It was for exactly $12.00. How I rejoiced! That meant more to me than if it had been twice that amount. The Lord spoke to me and said, "You didn't ask me for $12.00 in *your* mail; but in *the* mail." I got just what I asked for.

We were getting $25.00 a month from the Home Missions Department. I had rent to pay, four adults and a baby boy to feed, along with other expenses. Winter was coming, and I needed $10.00 to buy some winter clothing for my son. I did not have it, so I did the only thing I knew to do. I prayed and asked the Lord for it. That day a man came to my home and said he had met a friend of mine, who was passing through and didn't have time to stop. He wanted to send me $5.00 and asked this man if he would take it to me. The man brought the $5.00. Then he said, "I feel to put $5.00 with it." I had my $10.00

Later when I was leaving a church I had been pastoring, I needed $100 to pay a debt before I left. I did not want to leave with that debt not paid, so I prayed and asked the Lord to send me $100 by Monday morning. On Sunday a sister from a poor family gave me a bill. I put it in my pocket. Afterwards, when I got a chance, I looked at it and it was a hundred dollar bill. Never before had anyone given me a hundred dollars!

While in India a few years ago, I was booked to leave Madras at 7:00 o'clock in the morning. When I got to the airport, I was informed that my plane was delayed for needed repairs, that it would not be leaving until three in the afternoon. I left and came back around two. In response to an announcement that I did not understand I followed the crowd out of the waiting room, thinking it was my flight. When I showed my boarding pass, I was told that this was not my flight, that there was a further delay. (Incidently, my plane did not leave until five o'clock.) I went back to the waiting room, and to my dismay I saw that all the seats were taken. I had no where to sit down. I was very tired, having had only about three hours of sleep the previous night, plus a lot of traveling.

I stood for some time, my legs ached, and my back ached. Then I prayed, "Lord, You know how tired I am. Please give me a seat." Immediately a national got up at the other side of the waiting room, walked over to me and said, "You take my seat, and I will stand up." I sat there and talked in tongues under my breath and worshiped the Lord.

The Lord is wonderful. There are a lot of things I do not know, but this one thing I do know: God answers prayer.

Rev. A. W. Post.

Tent meeting days.

CHAPTER FOURTEEN

A Witness of God's Healing Power

by Ricky Robbins

My name is Ricky Robbins. I am sixteen years old and living in Spring, Texas.

I feel strongly that Jesus has a special calling for me. I have been healed of many afflictions in my short life.

At age ten I was diagnosed as having abdominal epilepsy and the doctors prescribed several medications, two of which I was told I would have to take for the rest of my life. I did take the medication for a couple of weeks. About this same time we visited my grandfather's house (Reverend Oliver F. Fauss) and I asked him to pray for me.

He took me into his office and called my grandmother (Sister Jewel Fauss). "Come in and pray for Ricky." In that big brown chair Jesus reached down and healed my body. Not even one time have I ever had the stomach pain again and I have never taken the medicine again. I know Jesus healed me.

When I was twelve years of age I became very ill. I was sent to go through Kelsey Seybold Clinic and then on to Texas Children's Hospital. After a week and a half of chaotic testing with several teams of doctors, it was explained to me that I had juvenile rheumatoid arthritis. This is why I could seldom walk a lot without falling down. My body would swell, especially my hands. At times I could not even hold a pencil to do my school work the pain was there constantly. I was to go daily for therapy, taking twelve pills a day. At first the pills helped some.

One day as I prayed, I told the Lord, "I cannot cope with pain any more. I want to go to school and do everything everyone else is doing." For the past year and a half my joints have not swollen. I give God the glory for this.

Since January thirty-first of this year, I have been in a body brace. I received two injuries to my back as a result of a fall from my motorcycle. I had two fractures shown already growing back. Since I have a high pain tolerance I had not seen a doctor at the time of the accident.

When my back began to hurt and swell two doctors immediately sent me to a specialist at the Medical Center in Houston. A doctor found that calcium was forming, and my lower vertebras were jammed, making it difficult for me to straighten up. It is a condition called Scheuermann's Disease which is usually found in elderly people. I was given a choice to wear a brace or have surgery. After about a year I would either be O.K. or would continue treatment. I was to be re-evaluated then.

I know that Jesus was with me again. I chose the brace because I knew He would help me bear the pain. I am used to it now and it is working. On my last check-up the doctor said he had not seen such progress in such a short period of time. People keep remarking, "Ricky, you sure are getting tall all of a sudden." I know that it won't be long until I am out of this brace for good. Things have just always happened to me like this and Jesus has always been there to guide my every step.

During the past few weeks, I have prayed often for God to have His way in my life. I have asked Him to guide me in all that I do. I want to be obedient to Him above all. I have felt very strongly that my life is a witness to the healing power of Jesus.

I would also like to tell you a most unusual case history documented at Baylor College of Medicine. Many people already know about how Jesus completely removed a living parasite that had eaten a hole through the cornea of my eye and how He destroyed all traces and restored completely the sight to my eye. If by telling of His miracle it helps only one person to have faith in the healing power of Jesus, then to me, it will have been worth it all.

In the summer months of 1974, I began to have pain in my right eye. It became swollen and red. Our family doctor sent me to several other doctors. They could see that something was wrong but no one seemed to know what. This was the beginning of many trips to the Medical Center for a very long period of time. I was seeing the head of Ophthalmology at Baylor College of Medicine.

It was discovered that I had something that no other person had been known to have. A parasite had entered into my blood stream and instead of dying as millions that we inhale every day do, this one started to grow behind my eye. By magnifying it thousands of times, the doctors could watch as it ate through the cornea of my eye.

I could barely see. Once I sat for hours as eighty-six doctors looked at my eye. As they lined up, I found that some of them were from different parts of the world. Each was here to see this worm that was living in my eye.

In trying to save my eye and destroy the parasite, the doctors sent my blood samples and other data to the Medical Research Center in Atlanta, Georgia. They were trying to find something that would kill the parasite and not harm me.

Each time I went for my visit to Baylor they made photographs which they magnified thousands of times. They used these pictures for future research and medical history. My mother also got to see the worm.

During this time my parents stopped attending church regularly. More and more they crowded God out of our lives. But my mother always prayed, no matter what. At night when I would say my prayers, I would ask God to help my mother and dad go back to church.

On Monday May 18, 1975, the doctors scheduled me for surgery. On Sunday my mother and dad talked it over, telephoned Brother Orlin R. Fauss, and asked if they could bring me to church Sunday night for prayer. I was excited and happy that we were going to church to have my Uncle Orlin pray for my healing. Greater Bethel Tabernacle was on Irvington Boulevard then. I remember that "Paw Paw" Fauss (Reverend O. F. Fauss) was there.

When the service started I wondered when they were going to pray for me. At the time, I did not know that Jesus was already speaking to Brother Orlin R. Fauss and telling him how to do it. Right in the middle of the service my Uncle Orlin came back to our pew and motioned for my mother and me to come out. Standing in the middle of the aisle, he laid hands on my mother and she begin to speak in tongues as God filled her with the Holy Ghost. He then prayed for God to have His way with me. I knew that Jesus had healed my eye.

The next morning as I jumped out of bed to get ready to go to the doctors, I realized that I could see. My mother said, "O.K. Ricky, but let's wait and see what the doctors have to say about it."

But my dad had me put something over my good eye as he held his fingers up. "How many fingers do you see, Ricky?" He would get all sorts of objects for me to prove to him that I could see. I knew Jesus had healed my eye and everything was going to be all right. My eye didn't even hurt.

At Baylor, the team of doctors got the machines ready to see the position of the parasite. I just sat and waited. The one setting up the machine seemed to have trouble adjusting the machine. They all tried. I wanted to tell them of my healing, but my mother told me to wait and hear the doctor.

When Dr. Danny Jones came in to see what was happening, I told him, "There isn't anything to see." They made the usual pictures of the eye; to their astonishment they found a perfect eye. There was not a scar, there was not a hole in the cornea, and the parasite was no longer there. I then told the doctors that I was prayed for and that Jesus healed my eye. The doctor said that it is a miracle. They only regretted that if anyone else were to have this same thing, they still did not have a cure.

This miracle happened in my day, in my generation, and in this church. Jesus performs miracles today, and I am a living witness.

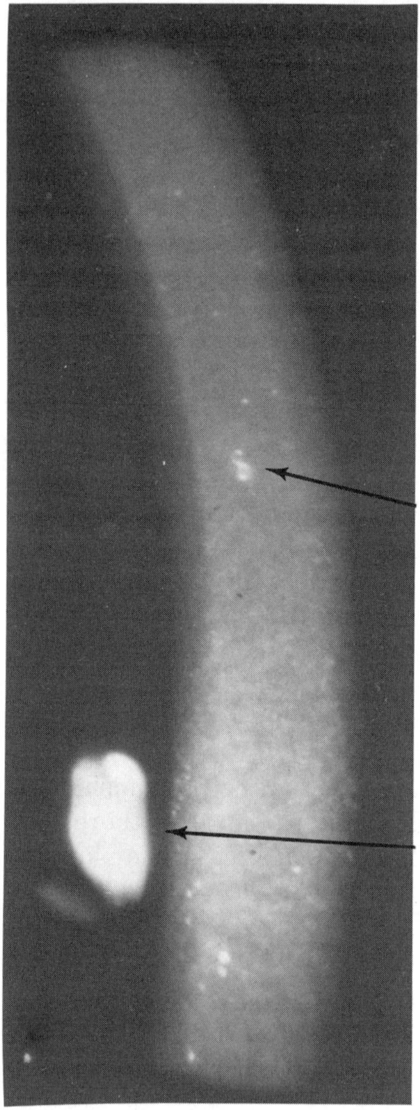

Ricky Robbins, Houston, Texas.

Parasite.

Eaten away by parasite.

CHAPTER FIFTEEN

Testimonies Of Healings by God

by E. L. Johnson

It is a great pleasure for me to bring you these testimonies of the healings I have seen done through prayer and fasting. God is a great God, and His power is great; His desire has always been to bless humanity.

In the state of Kentucky a pastor rented a Baptist Church building and was trying to bring in a new work. He wrote and asked if I would preach a revival for him. After a few days of prayer, I felt it would be the will of God for me to go. The pastor explained that it would be a missionary endeavor, but since I felt God had set His approval on our going I was not worried about the finance of the revival.

When we arrived, the pastor and his wife welcomed us and took us to the place where we were going to stay during the revival.

After unloading the car we sat down and discussed the plans for the revival. Then the pastor said, "Brother

Johnson, I failed to tell you in the letter that you and I and our wives are the only Pentecostals here."

Then a question ran through my mind: "Did God really put His approval upon my coming almost four hundred miles and only four Pentecostals—the pastor and his wife, my wife and I?"

It seemed that God gave another message to me: "Son, you are to work for Me in faith, not in the material blessings set before you. You must trust Me. You must believe that I will reward you if you will exercise your faith."

"Lord, I'll do it," I promised.

The pastor further stated, "The revival has been well announced throughout the community, but I don't know how well it will be attended. This community is made up of Baptists, Methodists, and Episcopalians."

This statement did not build up my faith, but it caused me to stand on what the Lord had said: "I will reward you if you will exercise your faith." So I did believe God. Here is what happened.

To our surprise, as the first service began the church filled to capacity with Episcopalians, Baptists, and Methodists. And the Lord blessed that very first night of the revival. There was such a godly atmosphere in the building that everyone desired to come back nightly.

About the fifth night of the revival as we entered the church with the pastor and his family, we saw a woman sitting on the piano bench. She got our attention and asked for Sister Johnson to come to her. She said to Sister Johnson, "I am Baptist but I have an affliction I would like for your husband to pray for. Would you ask him for me?"

"I will, but I think you should ask him," my wife replied.

Later she asked me, "Will you pray for me tonight?"

"I sure will. Could you tell me what your trouble might be?" I answered.

"Brother Johnson, I am a baldheaded woman. I don't have any fine hair anywhere on my head. I am completely bald with a shiny head. Do you suppose God will grow me another head of hair?"

"All things are possible with God," I assured her.

"Will you also pray for my mother? She is totally blind," the woman asked.

"Sure, I will pray for any one who may need prayer," I declared. Then I began to think on the experiences of the past. I could not think of any one that I had prayed for who was bald. "Oh, God, I really need You," I prayed. Then I remembered that God had told me His approval was on my coming here, so I reminded God that He had told me not to look at the material blessing but have faith and He would reward me.

As the service progressed, this lady and her mother were called to the front to be prayed for. As they stood, a halo of light encircled all of us. This moved all my doubt away. I knew God was going to reward me for going to help in this missionary endeavor.

I called the mother to come forward. I put my hand under my tie and asked, "Mother, tell me what color tie I have on?"

"Sir, I do not see you much less the tie. I don't even see the lights in this building."

With a simple prayer I asked God to open her eyes and let her see. Then I slipped my hand under my tie again and asked, "Now, can you tell me the color of the tie I am wearing?"

"I sure can. You are wearing a blue tie with red roses in it."

"Praise the Lord! You are right," I replied. Then I turned her toward the audience and asked, "Do you see any one in the audience that you know?"

She looked across the building. "I see my son whom I have lived with for the past six years and this is the first time I have seen him since I moved into his house."

Let me pause and say praise the Lord for opening the blind eyes, for the Lord is great and is greatly to be praised.

Then the lady with no hair on her head was next. I asked her if she would believe that the Lord would answer my prayer.

"If you say God will heal me and grow me another head of hair, I will believe and wait for it to grow," she replied firmly.

Another simple prayer was made but it was prayed from the heart and not the lips only. However, we did not see the hair immediately. But on the third night after she received prayer, as she was sitting before the mirror preparing herself for service, she started to place her fine wig, which had cost her eleven hundred dollars, on her head. Suddenly she noticed that some fine hair had started to grow. She was very happy and declared that she really believed the Lord was going to give her a full head of hair again.

Three years later at a General Conference we saw the pastor. He asked, "Do you remember the lady who had no hair?"

"I sure do," I replied.

Then he said, "That woman's hair has grown way below her waist, and now she is telling everywhere that the Lord grew her a new head of hair!"

Again I thank the Lord for what He did. Here is another great healing the Lord did that I would like to share. It happened in Crowley, Louisiana, in a United Pentecostal church service. The service had begun and the choir and testimonies had finished. The time had come for the preaching of the Word.

A woman who was visiting her relatives and had come to church arose from her pew and walked down the aisle to the pulpit. "I would like to be prayed for. There is a growth on my face and it happens to be a cancer, but I believe if I am prayed for now in this service that the Lord will heal me."

All faith and attention was directed to the lady's request. As we begin to pray, the power of God moved in and touched the lady. Three days later that growth fell off her face. Again we can give thanks to the King of kings and the Lord of lords for His mighty healing power.

Another lady in Jennings, Louisiana, came to a revival where I was preaching. She stated that she wanted God to heal her of a broken wrist and broken fingers, injuries she had sustained in an accident. She questioned the faith of the ministers and church, but we assured her that if she would believe, the Lord would heal her.

As prayer was being made unto the Lord, I requested, "Raise your arm."

"It's too sore! I am not able to raise my arm," she answered. But through the power of the name of Jesus, she began slowly to raise her arm until it was straight up in the air.

"Turn your wrist and move your fingers," I continued.

"The Lord has healed my fingers, my wrist and my arm," she declared. She began to use her arm and hand that very night. Then she cried aloud, "Oh, the Lord has completely healed me."

She testified to others of what the Lord had done for her and gave all the praise to the Lord.

I feel we should preach faith more often and encourage people to trust the Lord and prove His power. In some of the churches where I have conducted revivals I have had a few individuals come to me wondering if God really heals. I would try to convince them that God was the same to every one, and what He would do for one person He will do for others. But they did not have confidence God would heal them. This is one of the reasons I think we should stress faith to our congregation.

At a rural church between the towns of Jonesville and Harrisonburg, Louisiana, a lady came to church one Sunday morning walking on crutches. And after the morning worship had ended, she came forward and desired the church to pray for her that she would be delivered from her crutches. She stated, "I have been on these crutches for fifteen years, but I believe God will deliver me."

There were several ministers there that morning and all of us gathered around her and began to pray. The power fell, and she began to dance in the Holy Ghost with her arms lifted toward heaven. As she lifted her arms toward heaven, the crutches fell from under her arms. She danced off the platform shouting, "The Lord has delivered me from having to use the crutches to walk."

From that day until this she has not used the crutches again. She is still saying, "Hallelujah to the King of kings and the Lord of lords."

I give to God the glory of all He has done! To God be the glory.

CHAPTER SIXTEEN

The Wicked Flee When No Man Pursueth

by Marion Elizabeth Pietz

He's dead now!

He was shot down by a Houston, Texas, police department S.W.A.T. team.

If it were not for the fact that it really happened, it would have seemed just like another bad dream in the life of Jan Johnson. As a child, Jan was always prone to have vivid, life-like dreams—dreams that could be so beautiful that she wouldn't want them to end and yet dreams so frightening that Jan would wake up screaming and crying for her parents. Now, as she stood looking into the eyes of her attacker, Jan kept repeating to herself. "This is not a bad dream. It's really happening to me!"

It was just another typical Monday morning for Jan. She saw her husband off to work, watered her plants, put a load of laundry in the washer and then sat down to finish some work on a college course she was taking. Jan only stopped her routine long enough to prepare her fourteen-month-old daughter's breakfast. Jan remembers hearing noises at her front door, but she thought that it was nothing. Her neighbor had promised to stop by that morning for a cup of coffee and some fellowship. When she heard the knock at the front door, she picked her daughter up in her arms, went to the door and didn't stop to ask, "Who's there?"

The only person Jan expected to see standing on the other side of the front door was her neighbor. But, there he stood with a revolver in hand, a stocking covering his face and pushing his way into Jan's house and into her life.

In recalling her story, Jan remembers that she constantly called upon the name of Jesus. Growing up in a Pentecostal home, Jan was well taught from a very early age the power of the name. Praying in the name of Jesus was something Jan found very easy to do. It was just as easy and routine to pray in Jesus' name as it was to breath. Many times in her life, she had prayed for different personal requests and needs calling upon the name of the Lord. She prayed in the name of Jesus when she was about to get married, when she and her husband started their own business, and especially on the day when her first daughter was born. But Jan never prayed the way she prayed that day. For the intruder had come to rape and to kill. And, he was determined!

As he pushed his way in the front door, Jan let the door swing open wide and, still with her daughter in her arms, made a dash for the streets. With a quick turn, the intruder managed to grab her by the arm. He dragged her back into the house. Her once lovely home in an upper-middle class neighborhood had now become a threatening place of terror. A place of potential physical abuse and death.

Her attacker was big and strong, she was small and weak, Jan thought. "I don't stand a chance." Dragged back into the house Jan managed to run to the laundry room and the back door, only to be stopped by her intruder's harsh command, "Freeze, or I'll kill you!" Despite all her cries for help no one heard or saw anything. However, all during the ordeal Jan kept praying, "Jesus! Jesus!" So even if no one else heard her, Jesus did!

Her attacker stood but a foot away from her holding the revolver to her head. He demanded that she take her daughter to the other side of the house. Jan knew that this meant absolutely no chance of escape. "No matter what," thought Jan, "I must avoid that part of the house." As long as she was by the laundry room door there was still some hope of escape.

Jan boldly refused his command. They continued to stare at each other until suddenly, Jan Johnson realized, perhaps for the very first time in her life, that she was a child of the King of kings. And being His child she possessed a power much greater and stronger than the devil she faced. It was a power stronger than beatings, abuse, rape and even death itself. It was the power of the name of Jesus. The name that she had kept repeating over and over again. So, unlike any other time in her life, Jan faced this devil with all power given to her. She rebuked him saying, "In Jesus' name!"

As Jan stared at her attacker, there followed a brief moment of uncertainty. Then she noticed a doubt, a fear come into her attacker's eyes. Looking oddly about the room he became more and more uneasy with his situation. Then suddenly he asked Jan, "Lady, do you have a back door? I've got the wrong house."

He was defeated. He knew it and Jan knew it. Now, all he wanted to do was to get out of that house as quickly as possible. Why?

Did he begin to feel the power and presence of the King? Did he come face to face with a host of angels dispatched to defend a child of God? Well, whatever it was that he felt or saw in that laundry room, it was enough to make him want to flee for his life.

As he tried to threaten Jan to future silence, telling her he'd be back if she told the police, Jan's Holy Ghost boldness increased and she then demanded that he leave. And that he did very quickly, scaling a six-foot fence in one quick leap. "He ran like a man running away from someone who was chasing him," said Jan.

Exactly six months later, the attacker killed his wife, barricaded himself inside his house, and was eventually killed by the police.

When Jan is asked now to sing in church, her favorite song is, "The Beauty of His Name." To those of us who know her story, we understand how she must be feeling when she sings these words:

At the sound of His name every demon has to flee.
For to that name all power is given,
  to set the helpless captive free.
Every sin, disease, and sickness
  must bow down to that name.
And forever more surrender,
For all of time I shall proclaim.

Is it any wonder why that song is her favorite? Sister Jan Johnson lived that song!

Sister Jan Johnson, Porter, United Pentecostal Church.

CHAPTER SEVENTEEN

Divine Appointment

by Terry Hoffman, as told to Daniel Segraves

I was driving to work in Granite City, Illinois, when I stopped to pick up a couple of hitchhikers along Route 157. It was a rainy night, and the normally crowded highway was nearly deserted.

As one of the men climbed into the back seat, I heard a harsh voice behind me.

"This is a hold-up. I want all your money!"

As though to make absolutely sure his intention was clear, the backseat passenger hissed, "This is a real gun, and I want all your money right now!"

The other hitchhiker, who had slid into the front seat beside me, now menacingly pointed a switchblade to reinforce the threat.

A deathly fear gripped me, pumping adrenalin through my body. My hands felt glued to the steering wheel.

The spokesman for the pair continued, "Give me your

money or I'll blow you away right now!"

"Dear God, I have nothing! You've got to help me *now!"* I prayed, for after kissing my wife goodbye I had left home without my wallet, change, watch or pocket knife. All I had was my lunch and keys.

I thought I had prayed silently, but the robber barked, "Shut up and don't talk to anybody!"

However, the tide already had turned. From the moment I called on the Lord, a peace and calm had flowed through me, steadying my heartbeat, relaxing my knees and legs and returning my voice to normal. This inner strength was to keep me alive during the harrowing minutes that followed.

Again, the pair demanded money. Calmly, I said, "You're not going to believe this, but I left my house without a dime. All I have are my keys and lunch box."

The man with the knife searched me. Finding nothing, he said, "Let's kill him now."

"No," the other responded. "Let's take him out of town first."

They instructed me where to go. Enveloped in the God-given calm, I began to question my captors.

"What do you need money for? Are you sick? Hungry? Do you have bills? Do you need a fix?"

There was no response.

"Look," I ventured, "I'll let you out and forget the whole thing!"

Still no answer.

Another idea came to my mind. "You take my car and let me out. Go and do what you want to."

Again, there was no reply.

Then I began to ask my two passengers about their

relationship with Jesus Christ.

"Look, shut up with all this Jesus talk," the man in the back seat almost shouted. "He never did anything for a warlock like me!"

He then turned to his buddy. "Get a load of this guy!" he said, sarcastically. "He's about to die and all he can do is try to convert us!"

Following their commands, I entered a subdivision. Progress seemed aimless. . .left. . .right. . .left. . .almost as though my captors were stalling.

A second time, I made an effort to share God's willingness to help them and the fruitlessness of the life they were leading.

"Shut up with all the lectures! You're the only one that's in trouble! You've got to get us some money tonight or you're a dead man!" the back-seat passenger snarled as he thrust the gun barrel deeper into my neck.

An idea slowly formed in my mind. We were driving through a residential area at a snail's pace. The car nosed to a stop sign. Accelerating ever so gradually, I stealthily cracked my door, planning to leap out and run. I hadn't counted on the courtesy light, which immediately illuminated the interior of the car and exposed my plan.

An instant later, an ear-splitting *snap!* from the click of the hammer hitting the firing pin shattered the breathless silence. I knew I was dying, and waited for the blood and pain.

Then the realization that the gun had not gone off flooded me with sweet relief.

"Thank you, Jesus!" I exclaimed with a great sigh.

"If I'd had a better gun, you'd be dead now," the cold voice from behind warned. "So don't try anything again!"

Made bold by the peace and release from death, I said, "It wasn't the gun. It was God that caused it to misfire!"

As the automobile left the subdivision, another possible course of action formed in my mind. The only place I would have a chance of obtaining cash at this time of night would be my mother and father's home. There was no money at my house, and my wife was there alone.

"My dad may have $150 to $200," I suggested.

The robbers accepted the idea, and I turned the car in the direction of my parents' home. Then my mind began to whirl with doubts. What if they weren't home? What if they had company? Was I putting the lives of several people in danger? Would the desperadoes kill us all?

Suddenly a three-car accident loomed before us. Police cars were grouped with lights flashing and sirens screaming.

Tension mounted at this unexpected complication. Only one lane was open, and it seemed certain that I would have to stop the car.

The gun was cocked once more, as the voice grated, "Don't try anything or I'll kill you dead!"

"There's no way you could get away with it!" I protested. "There are three police cars here!"

"That's all right. I'll get you, and there's a bullet in this gun for me, too!"

Then, almost as though by a miracle, I was able to manuever the car straight through the middle of the police. We continued toward my parents' home on the outskirts of town.

Turning into their drive, I was surprised by a question from the gunman.

"Are your parents Christian, too?"

"Yes."

As we left the car, the gun never veered from my head. The knife-wielding member of the team stayed in the automobile.

Imagine my mother and father's shock when I appeared at their door at 11 p.m., with a gun in my back!

My father told the intruder that his money was in the bedroom. But he thrust the gun in dad's face and wouldn't allow him to leave the room.

My mother reached for her purse, and handed my captor about $25. Taking the money, the gunman started to take me hostage again. But a holy boldness seemed to rise up in Mom's spirit. She firmly told the robber to take the money and leave.

The three of us turned and, by the grace of God, began to edge our unwelcome guest toward the open door. Then, quickly, we backed him through the opening and slammed the door.

Later, after prayer and thanksgiving, we ventured out, and found no trace of either of the young men. The next morning, the police captured them in a local restaurant.

Some surprising facts later came to light.

Years before, the gunman, as a young lad, had purchased a horse from my father. He had come to our house weekly to make payments. We hadn't recognized each other, but as we turned into the drive he must have recalled the events of the more pleasant past.

Also, when the case came to court, a ballistics expert testified that the gun misfired on the same cylinder when test-fired about 100 times. You would never be able to convince me that the gun just happened to be on that cylinder by coincidence, when the attempt was made to kill me. Court testimony revealed that the gun had been stolen just before the robbery attempt, and the gunman knew nothing about its defective cylinder.

God must have had at least two reasons for sparing my life. Sure, He loves me. But He also loved my assailant enough to prevent him from blackening his record with murder; for God knew that the day would come when a letter from him would introduce us to a new member of His family.

When the letter arrived, my mother could not imagine who was writing her from a prison. But as she opened the envelope and read the contrite confession of wrong doing, the hopeful plea for forgiveness, and the sincere confession of a new faith in Christ, the events of that fateful night in March 1977 flooded her memory.

Reprinted by permission from Christian Life Magazine, November, 1981, Wheaton, Illinois.

Editor's Note: Terry Hoffman is a member of The First Pentecostal Church in Dupo, Illinois where Dan Segraves was pastor at the time this story was written. When I contacted Hoffman about the prisoner's current status, he told me that he had no further word from him but the last news was he was seeking the Holy Ghost.

CHAPTER EIGHTEEN

These Things And Greater

by O. T. Reynolds

This is the story of an automobile accident in which my daughter, Candy Canter, was badly injured and of the series of miracles which followed. It is written for the glory of God. The people mentioned are only mirrors whereby His glory is reflected.

I will begin with my son-in-law, David Canter, and his recollection of the accident itself.

February 14, 1984, 2:00 a.m.

Screaming. . .screaming. . .as I woke up I became aware of someone screaming loudly. Where was I? I found myself on my hands and knees on what used to be the glass T-top of our car. On the inside. Then I remembered. We were returning to our home at Holloman Air Force Base, New Mexico, from my parents' home in Phoenix. I had driven part way and then Candy had taken over and I went to sleep. Now the car was upside down and

Candy was screaming and it was dark. I had to reach Candy. "Dear God, help me to get to her." When I touched her, she was all wet and sticky with blood. I tried to open my door. "Oh, Lord, it won't open. Jesus, help me!"

I looked for another way out. The hatchback was open! "Thank You, Jesus." I crawled out the back and ran to Candy's door.

I jerked at the door and it opened. I tried to move her but couldn't. She was hanging upside down by her seat belt. Seat belt! I ran back and crawled through the hatchback and unfastened the seat belt. She was bleeding badly. Quickly I crawled back out and ran to her door. All her weight was now on her head and neck with the seat belt off.

"Candy, can you help me get you out?"

"It hurts, I can't move."

"Oh, Jesus, please don't let her back be broken. Help me get her out without hurting her more." I pulled her out as carefully as I could. I put her down and saw that her scalp was peeled back and big patches of her skull were showing. "Jesus, help us." I started trying to flag down a car.

Several went by, not even slowing down. Then a big 18 wheeler slowed and stopped. The driver ran to help while his wife (husband and wife driving team) called for an ambulance on the C.B. We covered Candy up and propped her feet on a suitcase to try to prevent shock.

Praying constantly, I held her in my arms, trying to keep her quiet. When she screamed it scared me, but when she became still I was afraid she was dead. Finally the ambulance came. We arrived at a small hospital in Silver

City three or four hours after the accident.

• • • • • • •

On February 14 about 7:00 a.m. David called me at home in DeSoto, Missouri. "There has been an accident. Candy has been nearly scalped, and her skull is fractured in two places," he said. They were sending her by helicopter to the big William Beaumont Army Medical Center in El Paso, Texas, because of the skull fractures. I told him we would come to El Paso as soon as possible.

On the way to El Paso my wife and I stopped often to call the hospital. No change. Still critical. Praying. Miles. Still critical. No change. Hours. Miles. Dixie, my wife, asked the Red Cross worker who answered, "Do you know how to pray?" Silence.

"Why, yes. Yes, I do."

"Will you go in and pray for our daughter until we get there?"

"Certainly." No change. Hours. Miles. Still critical.

When we arrived, David's parents were there, staying up with him day and night. Candy was in intensive care, her head bandaged and eyes swollen shut. She was lying totally still. Can she hear us? They don't know.

"Candy, Mom and Dad are here. Squeeze our hands if you hear us."

"Did she?" asked Dixie.

"I don't know," I answered.

We went back out to the waiting room since we could only stay in the intensive care room a few minutes at a time. We took turns with David and Brother and Sister Canter as only two at a time were allowed. Although David was very tired, he wanted me to go with him to get quarters on the Army base. Then we came back to the waiting room where the Canters were encouraging Dixie. We waited but there was no change.

We had arrived at the hospital about 7:00 p.m. after driving for twenty-four hours. By midnight we were totally exhausted, so we all went to our rooms.

There is a large mountain just behind and to the left of the hospital. Just before I went to sleep, I seemed to see the mountain move quickly to the right. Moving mountains? Faith—the combined faith of hundreds of saints praying for Candy would bring her through. I woke Dixie and told her, but she just groaned.

By 6:00 a.m. we were back at the hospital. We asked David what the doctors were saying about the two skull fractures.

He gave us an odd look. "They can't find any skull fractures." *Miracle one.*

The doctors said that her brain was badly bruised and swollen. When David asked them what the effects of that would be, they answered, "She might have to learn things all over again."

"How long would this last?"

"It could be temporary or it could be permanent." They were not sure. "We'll just have to wait and see," they told us.

Later David came out of intensive care with his dad. David was grinning and Brother Canter was beaming.

"She squeezed my hand," says Brother Canter.

We hurried in. She was lying very still. I took her hands and told her we were there. "Do you understand? Squeeze my hand if you can hear me." She squeezed my hand.

As her mother was reading the Bible to her later in

the day, Candy whispered something. What? "Read Psalm 34." Tears filled our eyes. That was her favorite Psalm. Candy smiled! *Miracle two.*

We went back to the waiting room. Everyone was talking at once when the phone rang. Candy's twin sister was calling from Virginia, where her husband is stationed. Sandy was coming. Jack Lambrich, the father of a girlfriend of the twins in Hillsboro, Missouri, had sent her money to go from Virginia to El Paso and back so that she could be with Candy.

Betty Whayne, my wife's supervisor, called from World Evangelism Center. "How is Candy?" Then she said that the folks at headquarters thought we might be getting low on money, so they took up a little collection. She had deposited $740.00 in our account! A "little" collection? A big burden lifted. Good people. God's people.

David had to go back to the Army base to take care of some things and wanted me to go with him. We walked into their house and found the things Brother Canter had gotten out of the wrecked car. David showed me his and Candy's blood-soaked jackets and the blanket with huge splotches of blood all over it. There was blood on other clothes. As an ex-military policeman with some experience with such things, I estimated that at least three pints of blood had been lost. I asked David how much blood they had to give her when she got to the hospital.

He gave me a puzzled look. She had not needed a transfusion. None. We just stood and looked at each other past the bloody clothes. Was this *Miracle three?*

The plastic surgeons told us about trying to fix Candy's scalp when they brought her in. Candy had lost big patches of her scalp; there was one that was two inches wide from her forehead nearly to the crown. The surgeons had thought that they would have to do a lot of skin grafting, which would mean that she would have patches where hair would not grow. But they said they were amazed at their own work. They had somehow been able to pull her scalp together and sew it so that there were no spots where hair would not grow. They acted as though they couldn't believe it was possible. We believed it. Other hands had been at work in that operating room. God had been there. *Miracle four.*

Candy began talking a little. She told the nurse that she was thirsty.

"Oh, you will not be able to take anything on your stomach for at least five days," the nurse explained.

Candy just smiled like a child who knew that her Father was in charge. The next morning when we walked in, Candy was sitting up and eating breakfast. . .eating breakfast? And drinking juice and water.

We looked at the nurse. The nurse shrugged and spread out her hands helplessly. Candy pointed to the water and smiled. *Miracle five.*

But when we went in two mornings later, Candy seemed to have had a bad relapse. She was trying to eat breakfast but she could not put the food in her mouth. She moved her hand too fast and hit herself in the forehead.

"I can't. My hands won't do what my brain tells them." She continued to miss her mouth.

The doctor told us that she apparently had brain damage since her brain was bruised and badly swollen. "We will have to operate on her brain to reduce the swelling. The damage may be permanent," he said.

We were all shocked. Tears fell. She had been doing so well.

The next morning the doctors told David that they had discovered that Candy had too much medication in her blood. They had been giving her a relaxant type medicine that was supposed to pass on through her body, but she was retaining too much of it. They said that could be part of her coordination problem. David asked about the swelling in the brain. "It had started to go down for some reason."

She was now eating and moving normally. Too much medication? Brain swelling going down without an operation? No brain damage? All overnight? Or did God perform night time surgery? The doctors didn't know what to think. We knew. *Miracle six.*

Finally Candy was able to get up and be helped to the bathroom. She had not seen herself in the mirror. The bandages were now off and the stitches were all over her head. No hair. She was washing her hands when she glanced up. "What's that? Oh, that is me!" When she came out of the bathroom, she said, "I don't have any hair."

"That is the least of our worries," we assured her.

The doctors had told us that Candy would be in intensive care for at least one month and then would remain in the hospital for at least another two weeks. This was their initial timetable. God had a different timetable. On her tenth day in intensive care the doctors told her they were moving her to a regular room the next morning—one third of the time.

The day she moved into a regular room, she asked us to get her some pizza.

David asked the nurse if we could bring pizza into the room.

"It's against the rules, but go ahead."

Three days later they sent her home!

She was out of the hospital in less time than she was supposed to spend in intensive care! The doctor called it an amazing recovery. No. Amazing grace! *Miracle seven.*

Candy had to return to the hospital for checkups and one time for some minor surgery on one spot on her scalp. Her hair had grown about half an inch, but they had to shave it off again for the minor surgery. This was a low spot for her, because she wanted her hair back so badly.

One time while trying to arrange her wig for church, she told David she didn't want to style a stupid wig, she wanted to comb her own hair. David held her and told her she would soon be fixing her own hair. Later she got tickled and got over the blues.

When she returned to the hospital about a month later for her final checkup, the nurse asked her to remove her wig so they could check her. She was not wearing a wig. Her hair grew so fast that the nurse could not believe it. Hair growing at twice normal speed? A small thing to many, but to Candy it was *Miracle eight.*

Candy is now totally and completely healed. The doctors took pictures of her head from the first day for training films to show that seemingly impossible things could be accomplished. So they are still talking, when they show the films, about luck and surgical skill. They have to talk about what they know. And so do we. We will continue to talk about miracles.

> *"I will bless the Lord at all times! His praise shall continually be in my mouth" (Psalm 34:1).*

The Mountain

We looked upon our broken child
Lying still upon the bed.
We listened while they told us
Of the injuries to her head.
They said that she might never be
The girl we used to know.
Then a thousand saints began to pray,
A million tears did flow,
And two thousand hands reached out
By works their faith to prove.
Now mine eyes have seen the glory
I saw the mountain move.

We looked upon our child once more,
And for a little space
She lay still as death, and then
The blankness left her face.
She moved a little, and then I
Felt her squeeze my palm.
And she whispered to her mother
The number of a Psalm.
The doctors speak of luck and skill,
Her recovery to prove;
But I will speak of miracles,
I saw the mountain move.

o. t. reynolds

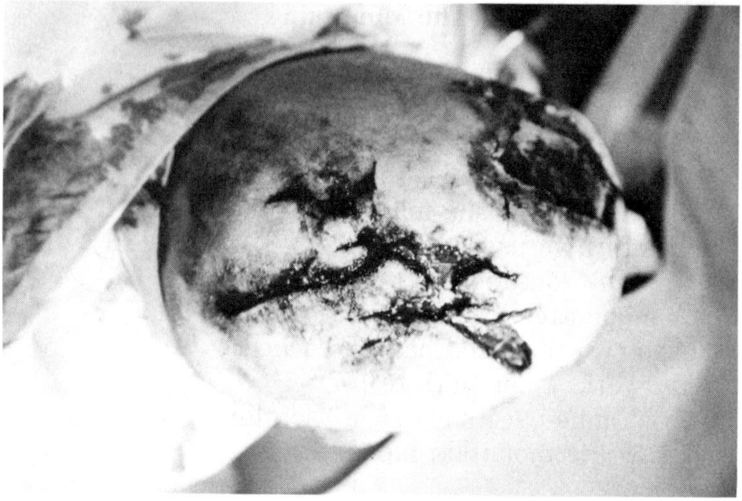

Skull Shot after wreck. Taken at William Beaumont.

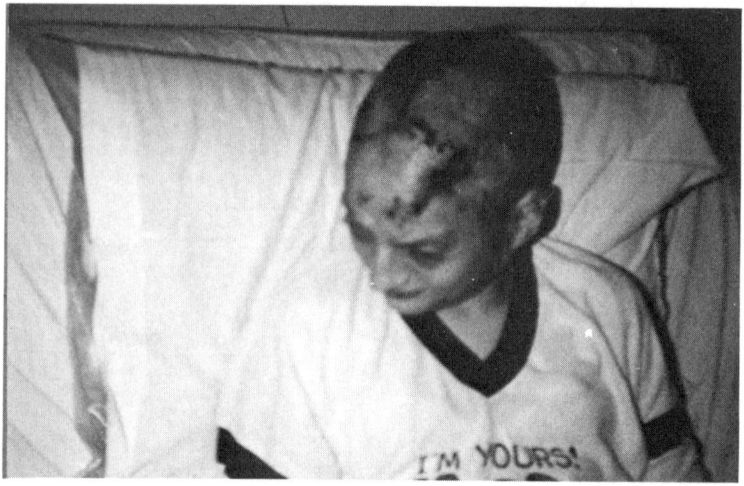

Twelve days after wreck.

Before the wreck, Candy and husband.

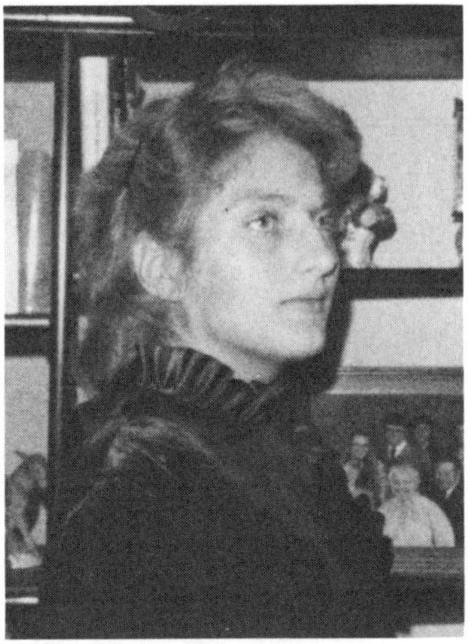

Look how my hair has grown, November, 1984.

Candy with her twin, Sandy at General Conference, 1984.

CHAPTER NINETEEN

The Miracle Of The Empty Highway

by Larry Vaughan as told to Frances Vaughan

The heavy traffic was moving freely as I maneuvered my pickup truck onto the freeway. "Good," I thought, "I've just enough time to reach the hospital before the five o'clock rush."

My truck swayed as I moved the steering wheel. Something about the way it handled niggled the back of my mind, but I was so intent on my troubles that I shrugged it off.

The low, dark-gray clouds and cold November drizzle matched my mood. My gloom deepened as I thought of the evening ahead. I was heartily sick of hospitals.

"Some Thanksgiving this is going to be," I muttered, visualizing my mom and dad with my little sister, enjoying dinner by a cozy fireplace, while my wife, Jan, and I were sitting in a hospital room with a cranky child.

I rubbed my throbbing knee. This dreary weather made it ache more than usual, but no amount of massaging could erase the pain, any more than it could erase the memory it evoked.

Eight months earlier I had a motorcycle accident and had broken six ligaments in my right leg. After restorative surgery and ten days in traction, I went home to look forward to long months of therapy.

At first, I was optimistic in spite of the intense pain and the fact that we had no money. Jan was expecting our second child, but we had a little insurance. Besides, God had taken care of our family for four generations. I had no reason to doubt He would continue to care for us.

Then one day I hobbled into the house and found Jan sitting at the kitchen table in her faded maternity dress, huddled over a pile of bills. She was weeping. I stood beside her, helpless. I prayed, but there was no miraculous answer.

That summer we had a hail storm. Hail stones as large as golf balls battered my truck and my mobile home. My red pickup truck was my pride and joy, but when we received the insurance settlement for the damage, we used the money to pay bills, instead of making repairs.

Now, seeing the dents accented on the wet hood in the fading afternoon light, I sank deeper into self-pity.

Our baby was born by Caesarian section in August. We were elated to have another beautiful daughter in the family, but our joy was quickly squelched by mounting medical and household bills.

Jan's recuperation seemed to take forever and I couldn't encourage her because I was so discouraged myself.

"God, where are You?" I questioned.

I hoped to go back to work in October, but my leg

wasn't straightening and the doctor wouldn't release me.

Our folks were tremendously supportive and helped financially as much as they could. I tried to swallow my pride, but it stuck in my throat and I hovered between gratefulness and helpless frustration.

By November things were looking up and I was beginning to hope again. Baby Brooke was thriving and I managed to do a few light jobs.

My parents gave us a Christmas present early—cash! It was hunting season, so Jan and I decided to treat ourselves to a camping trip. I thought it would be good therapy for both of us.

We left two-year-old Brenda and baby Brooke with Jan's parents, borrowed their camp trailer and went merrily on our way. The girls both had slight colds, but nothing alarming and we knew they would have the best of care.

By the time we made the long five-hour drive and set up camp, it was too late to do any hunting. We cooked supper and went to bed early, anticipating a good day tomorrow.

The next morning, Jan went to a nearby town to call her mother to check on the girls.

When I came back to camp at mid-morning, Jan was frantically packing the gear.

"Hurry, we've got to go home right away!" she shouted, "Brenda is in the hospital. She has pneumonia."

We arrived at the hospital at four p.m. Brenda looked terrible with huge dark circles under her eyes. It was frightening. Her temperature was 104 degrees and she appeared lifeless.

That was four days ago. She was out of danger at the

last doctor's report, but would have to spend several more days at the hospital. Although I was thankful Brenda was on the mend, I didn't look forward to spending the next week at the hospital.

The exit to the Cross-Town express was coming up, so I concentrated on maneuvering through the traffic. There was a propane truck on my right. He had been there for quite awhile. With my vehicle acting the way it was, I wanted to give him a wide berth. I didn't want to tangle with him on this wet pavement, so I slowed and fell behind the auto on my left.

Something was definitely wrong with my truck. It became more evident as I went into my turn. The front end visibly wobbled. It probably needed aligning.

"Oh, Lord," I thought bitterly, "What next? Do you even care?"

I came off the curving ramp onto the strangely deserted expressway. Then, all thought was driven from my mind as I struggled to control my pickup.

It lurched from one side of the road to the other. I fought for control. I dared not brake for fear of turning over. There was a scraping sound under the truck and I knew the tie-rod had fallen. I finally managed to get the truck to the shoulder and stopped.

Shaking, I climbed out to assess the damage. My legs felt rubbery and I gave a sigh of relief. The evening traffic resumed its heavy flow and I stared in amazement.

Something inside me began to bubble. A slow grin widened my face as it dawned on me what had taken place. An empty freeway doesn't happen at five o'clock in the evening without a miracle. Another miracle had taken place too—I wasn't alone anymore and what's more,

I realized God had been there all the time.

I stood in the drizzling rain with new confidence surging within. None of my problems had changed. In fact, I had a new one—a disabled truck. I would have to walk on a painful leg to find help. My child was still in the hospital. The bills were yet to be paid. But, I was alive and I felt good about it. I knew I could make it with God directing the traffic in my life.

CHAPTER TWENTY

Nine Machines And God

by *LaJoyce Martin*

"Mr. Martin. . ." The doctors could not meet my husband's searching eyes in the consultant room at the Scott-White Hospital. They looked at the floor.

Ninety miles away, I was kneeling beside the bed in the home of my parents, with a severe back injury. When the phone rang, my husband requested that my father tell me the sad news.

Our two daughters, sixteen-year-old Angela and fourteen-year-old Bethany, had started home from church in our small Audi on the night of the sixth. Angela, a fanatic about seat belts, had buckled up before leaving the parking lot. "I'll buckle up in a minute," Bethany promised, toying with a stereo cassette in the back seat. She never got the seat belt fastened.

On the well-lighted four-lane boulevard less than a mile from our home, Angela failed to turn on her headlights. A car rolled up beside her and blinked. She looked down to engage the lights on the downhill slope, and when she raised her eyes, she was dangerously close to the rear of the automobile ahead. Swerving to change lanes, she felt the car careen. Overcorrecting, she jerked the wheel the opposite direction, throwing the car into a fatal skid, and slid off the road into a large tree. Occupants of a passing vehicle heard the girls screaming and praying as the Audi jumped the curb sideways, flipped onto two wheels and bashed against the immovable object broadside. The tree lacked six inches plunging half way though the small car. The frame on the driver's side broke and the vehicle wrapped itself U-shaped about the tree, shattering glass in all directions.

My husband waited in agonizing uncertainty at the hospital. Angela would be all right he learned, but he was not allowed to see Bethany. At last the doctors came. "She's in a coma and hemorrhaging on both sides of her brain," they reported. "The brain itself is severely bruised. You can expect at least six months hospitalization. We are uncertain as to the extent of brain damage, and we are not sure we can save her right eye." In extreme critical condition, Bethany was sent to the Intensive Care Unit. Nine machines—and God—kept her alive.

I sensed that something was wrong when Mother took the extension phone around the corner so that I could not hear any of the conversation. Then I heard her call Dad. Feeling troubled inside, I asked what the problem was.

Soon Dad came to break the news as gently as possible. He touched the tips of his fingers together, "I don't know how to tell you this. . .but the girls have been in an accident."

"Which one was killed?" I asked bluntly.

"Angela is going to live, but they don't know about Bethany. . . ."

Dad waited, expecting my hysteria, sobs, desperation. "Dad," I said quietly, "I dedicated Bethany to the Lord when she was born. If He wants another angel in heaven's choir, then He'll give me grace and strength to bear my loss."

One of the hardest things I had ever faced in my life was not being able to see my injured child, to hold her inert hand, to talk to her unheeding little body. . .and the knowledge that if she died, I would not even be able to attend her funeral. My severe back injury had made me bedfast, and I suffered fifty-six days of torturous pain. I could not sit, stand or lie down without pain. The only relief I found was in a kneeling position.

For most of the night when we heard the news I prayed, not knowing how or what to pray, feeling a human helplessness I had never before experienced.

Bethany's short life flashed before my grief-stricken mind. A special child from birth, she had started reading through the Bible at five years of age. (She loved trying to pronounce the "begats" in the Chronicles.) To date she had read it through five times. Her intelligence was near college level. On the mantle at home sat the trophy she won for the highest grades in her large eighth grade class just two months ago. She played the piano and organ well. Her Christain witness at school impressed everyone. She joined the Joy Germs Club and she was one of the happiest children alive. And now. . . ?

Around 4:00 a.m., something welled up inside of me. Hope? Faith? Renewed strength? I called my husband at the hospital. "Honey," I said with feeling, "We need a miracle! Our church needs a miracle! Our city needs a miracle! God hasn't told us He's ready to take our Bethany, and until He does, it is our privilege to believe that He will give us one!"

The crisis came the following night. The doctor called my husband into the family counseling room. "Her brain is deteriorating," he said. "The blood vessels are giving way. . . .Our only hope will be brain surgery if the seepage cannot be stopped. And we may lose her. . . ." The doctor said that his wife was home praying for our daughter along with himself. "And I want to tell you how to pray specifically. Pray that the blood vessels in the brain stabalize."

Some fifty people joined the prayer. Special friends and neighbors, some who were not acquainted with prayer, knelt and asked God for the miracle. In one hour the report came that the process of deterioration had reversed itself. The leaking had stopped just short of the fatal loss of red blood cells.

My husband never left Bethany's side except to change clothes. Calls began to pour in from all over Texas and seventeen other states. Concerned people were praying everywhere. Doctors, nurses, neighbors, and people he did not know came with words of encouragement.

When the coma persisted into the second week, my husband's heart grew heavier and heavier. He moved to Bethany's side, and spoke gently in her ear, "Bethany, we're going to pray." As he asked God to bring her out of the coma, Bethany's lips began to move and she opened her eyes. She was praying, too.

On July 26, 1985, twenty days after her accident, Bethany walked out of the hospital with her carload of stuffed animals, sucker bouquets, and balloons. She went to church that night.

Her testing shows college level intelligence, her sense of humor and radiant smile are still in evidence, and her near-unsalvagable right eye has almost perfect vision. No scars. . .no disfigurement. . .no brain damage.

The insurance adjustor came to view the totally demolished car. "Angela's seat belt saved her," she said, "but had Bethany had her seat belt fastened, the impact would have killed her instantly."

God thinks of even the little details.

God watches over Angela and Bethany.

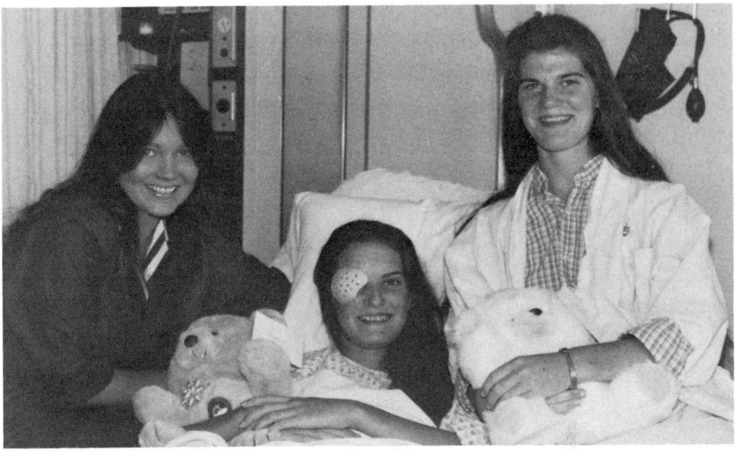

Friend Tammy Childress (lt) and Sister, Angela Martin (rt) come to visit Bethany the next day after she regained consciousness from the coma. Accident occurred July 6, 1985, picture taken July 21, 1985.

CHAPTER TWENTY-ONE

Through Long Lonely Nights, God Is There

by Mary Wallace

"Mary, has Jeff fallen and hurt his stomach? It's swollen tight as a drum." J. O. questioned me while he was bathing our small son one Saturday night.

"I don't think so. We are going to Doctor Bridges Monday. I'll have him check it."

This began a nightmare ordeal for the Wallaces. In 1955, J. O. and I were living in Nashville. He was co-pastoring the West Nashville United Pentecostal Church with his father. Jeff was the youngest child of our family at that time.

On Monday Doctor T. F. Bridges poked Jeff's tummy, asked questions, drew some blood, and then, said solemnly, "Come back tomorrow for a report on the blood work."

Later when my husband I were discussing the problem, the word *leukemia* crossed my mind, but I hastily shoved it out. The next day we returned for our appointment. "Reverend Wallace," Doctor Bridges cleared his throat. "Jeff, may have a serious blood disorder."

"Not leukemia," I interrupted.

"Well, I hope not, Mrs. Wallace, but of the three symptoms of the disease, he has two. His liver is enlarged. That's what caused the swollen stomach and his white cell count is up. Now, I want to do a bone marrow. Let's check him in the Baptist Hospital and see if this thing shows up in the bone marrow."

"Today?"

"I want it done as soon as possible," the doctor said seriously.

"But we need to take him home to get pajamas and stuff. Can't we wait until tomorrow," I urged. (What I really wanted was to get home and have Papa J. W. Wallace pray for our son.)

Soberly and silently we drove to the duplex we shared with Papa and Mama Wallace; there we had a good season of prayer. Then my husband began to phone friends to ask for more prayer. We lay sleepless through the long, lonely night.

The next morning, we checked our small boy into the hospital. Always grinning and cutting up, Jeff was worried least of all of us and marched off bravely for his bone marrow. Later he returned to the room quite pale and not grinning anymore. (A bone marrow test is not funny. That big needle is forceably pushed right through the bone.) At last we said good night and returned home to wait for the test results the next day.

Another long, lonely night passed filled with tears and prayers. We hurried back to the hospital early the next morning for the final word.

A smiling doctor gave us great news. "The bone morrow test was negative. Jeff can go home," Doctor Bridges answered.

"That's great, Doctor. We felt sure that God would hear our prayers."

"Well, it must have been a Higher Power. He had all the classic symptoms of the disease." The doctor shook his head perplexed.

"Then what caused the swollen stomach?" we asked.

"I have no idea."

But we knew. God had stopped the dread disease of leukemia because we know God answers prayer. The stomach, however, remained swollen.

Years later in 1964 we went back to prayer again for Jeff. Brother and Sister C. M. Becton, J. O. and I were invited to speak at a Sunday school meeting in Toronto, Canada. I had left my mother, Maria Hardwick, in charge of our six children and our school, West Nashville Kindergarten and Nursery. Rosemary and Joe were born after the story above.

"Be careful, children. Mind Grandma. We'll be home in a week." My mother was a teacher in the school and a very responsible person fully qualified for the responsibility of running a large school of one hundred preschoolers as well as watching after our six.

We flew into Toronto and went on to the church for the first meeting. As we sat in the service, the church phone began to ring. R-r-ring! Over and over the phone rang, then it finally was silent.

The service was lengthy and it was after 10:00 p.m. before we returned to the parsonage. As we drove into the garage, the phone was ringing in the parsonage. The pastor hastened to answer. "It's for you, Brother Wallace—long distance." My heart stood still.

J. O. answered, "Hello, what? What happened, Alton? Yes, well, do what you can. Let me see what we can do. I'll call you back." He hung up the phone quietly.

"What's wrong?" I asked.

"It's Jeff. He fell thirty feet out of a tree, broke his arm, messed up his face and they think he has internal injuries. His stomach is swollen and they want to operate. That was Alton (my brother-in-law). He says the doctor needs permission to operate."

"Let's pray. God can touch Jeff," Brother Becton said quietly. We began to call on God.

Then Brother Wallace called the airport to see about passage home. "What, none at all. No more flights to the states until in the morning." My heart sank! My child was hurt and I was over a thousand miles away from home.

"But, J.O., the swollen stomach may not indicate internal injuries. You know his liver has stayed enlarged somewhat since that time that God touched him when Doctor Bridges thought he had leukemia," I reminded my husband.

"Yes, that's true! Well, we'll have to trust God again. I'll call Alton and O.K. the surgery if they feel they must operate," he said as he turned to place the call.

Another long, lonely, miserable night filled with tears and prayers.

Early the next morning we placed the call. "Hello, Alton, how is Jeff? Great! The doctor didn't have to operate! Wonderful! Yes, I know. God *does* answer prayer."

"He's fine, Mary. Our boy is all right. They have set

his arm and sewed up his face. Most of the stitches were in his mouth. Alton says Jeff's main concern is that he has spoiled our trip. There are twenty or so relatives visiting him and he does *not* want us to cancel here."

God does answer prayer! When you raise six children you really do rely on a prayer-answering God.

Then in 1971 we desperately needed that prayer-answering God again. Our children, Margie, Rosie and Joe were driving Margie's new Plymouth Satellite from Nashville to St. Louis. Outside Carmi, Illinois, a speeding driver nudged her off the highway then sped on. When she tried to pull back on the highway, the right front wheel broke, causing her to lose control of the car. The car turned over two or three times, coming to rest on its top by a telephone pole.

A few minutes earlier she had suggested, "Rosie, let's turn the air off and roll the window down. Joe's asleep in the back and we can enjoy the breeze." When the car finally stopped careening, Rosie was thrown out but just barely. Her hand was actually caught under the car but she was able to pull it clear.

Margie crawled out her window crying hysterically, "Where's Joe?" She thought he was trapped under the car.

Passing automobiles brought help. They found Joe unconscious under the back seat. "His leg's broke," was the first diagnosis. "Call an ambulance!" They rushed the children to a clinic in Carmi.

"This boy will need to go to Evansville to the hospital. He may need brain surgery," the local doctor declared after a brief examination.

Meanwhile Margie tried to reach us at World Evangelism Center in St. Louis, but Virgie Miller, the switchboard operator, could not understand the hysterical voice on the phone. Finally Rosie took the phone and explained to Virgie what had happened.

Brother Wallace and I were at the hospital visiting a sick friend, but Virgie found us. "I'll call the airport while you pack. Call Jim (our oldest son who was working in St. Louis at the time)." Again we stormed heaven with our prayer.

"Mary, we can't get a plane out until 5:00 this afternoon. Let's drive! We can drive to Evansville by 5:00. Now I must talk to the neurosurgeon at Evansville hospital. He wants permission to do brain surgery. Then I want to call my minister friend, Brother Ray Miles. He can go to the hospital and pray with the kids."

Soon we were rushing east. "It's been an hour or so, J. O. Let's stop and call the hospital. I just feel like God has undertaken."

The call was placed and the news was better. "The doctor's not going to operate for awhile. We'll call again in a couple of hours." When we got to Carmi, Jim said, "Let's stop and see if we can find the car, Dad." Soon we drove into the garage where the car had been pulled.

"Oh, no! Oh, dear God, how could they still be alive. Jim, that car is demolished." And it was. The roof of the car was flat on the top of the seats. How had they managed to escape! They should have been decapitated.

Back into the car we piled, very concerned, praying, as the miles rolled by. There was the hospital. Quickly we parked, hurried into Emergency and was directed to the Intensive Care Unit where we met the doctor in charge.

"We think your boy is going to be all right, Reverend

Wallace. His leg is not broken. He's regained consciousness and we are just going to watch him here in Intensive Care for tonight."

Later Margie told us, "Mom, it was awful. I thought I had killed Joe. I don't know how Rosie and I got out alive. My long hair was filled with glass. My shoes were tied on my feet and were knocked off somewhere in the wreckage. On the ride in the ambulance Joe kept vomiting and he was unconscious. I thought he was gonna die. I was sitting in front by his head and Rosie rode by him. But when we got to the hospital Brother Miles was here and he prayed for Joe in Emergency. Then Joe opened his eyes for the first time!"

Brother and Sister Miles were still there to comfort us and pray with us. He told my husband, "I have rented a room here at a nearby motel for you. Let me know if there is anything else we can do. But Brother Wallace, God has touched Joe." Peace filled our hearts.

At eleven p.m. we were allowed in Intensive Care for the last time. "Yes, nurse, I know I can't visit him through the night, but I will be here in the waiting room. If he needs us, we'll be here praying." Another long, lonely night of vigil but God was near.

Early the next morning we were allowed to see Joe briefly. "I'm fine," Joe smiled at us. So we left the hospital to go to the motel to rest.

Hand in hand we walked across the parking lot with peace in our hearts. As the sun rose, I turned to J. O. "God is so good. He's always there to help us. Just think, we could just as easily have been choosing three caskets today but instead we can check Joe out of the hospital and go back to St. Louis all together."

"Yes, Mary, God is good. He's a prayer-answering God," my husband said firmly.

We've spent many a long lonely night in prayer for other needs since then, but we still say, "God answers prayer."

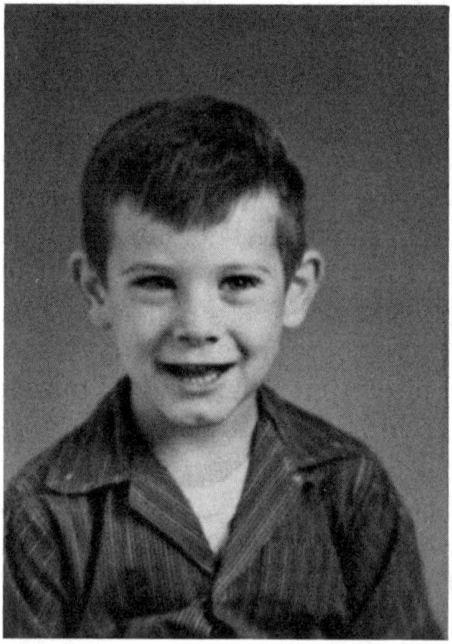

Jeff Wallace at age five, with possible leukemia.

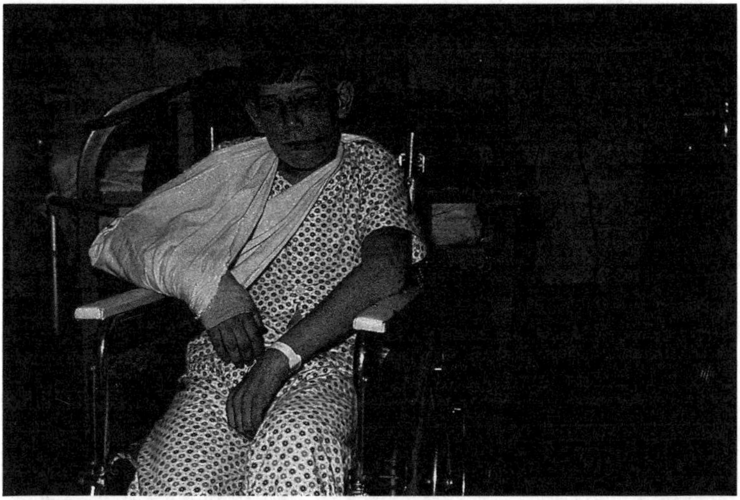

Jeff Wallace after fall from tree.

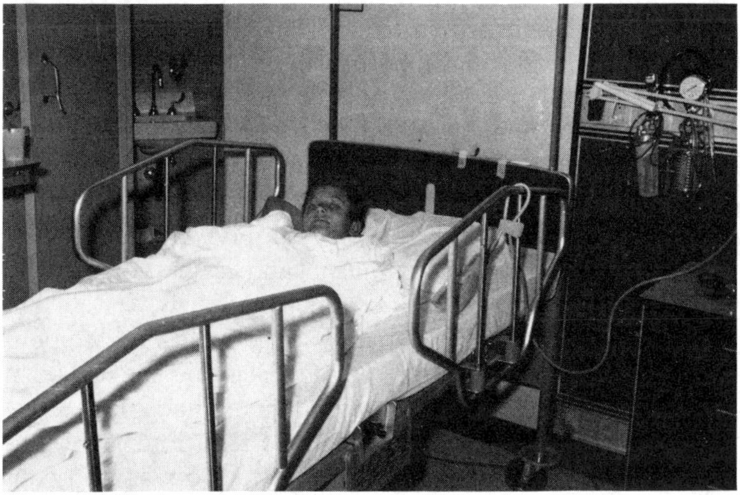

Joe Wallace in Intensive Care at Evansville.

Margie's car was totaled. The Lord does watch over us.

CHAPTER TWENTY-TWO

Truck in Trouble

by Bill Hughes

Monteagle is a small city in Tennessee with a population of about one thousand. It is located fifty miles west, northwest, of Chattanooga on the southern end of the Cumberland Plateau.

The city sets atop a ridge, which is crossed by Interstate 24 and other highways. This ridge is known by truckers and local residents as Mt. Eagle Mountain. Tourists are often shocked to find themselves climbing this ridge because there is nothing recorded on maps to indicate a mountain. It is about a five mile climb from the bottom to the top.

Most truckers are aware of its dangers and have great respect for it. The east side going down is the steepest with a couple of bad curves. Many times, truckers who are not familiar with this area wind up in deep trouble. Going east, the highway is a regular four lane interstate. When you reach the top, the highway splits and you descend downward on the old U.S. 41 road bed, which becomes a three lane.

I have crossed this mountain many times during my twenty-six years as a professional driver. I have seen the remains of many trucks that have crashed in and around the "big cut," which is about two-thirds the way down. The highway there is always scarred and rough, caused by grinding metal. Very few truckers have survived these crashes. Some drivers have tried jumping from their rigs only to be crushed beneath their own wheels.

In 1976 a sand pit was built for run-away trucks. It is located just to the right of the "big cut." I never dreamed I would ever have to use it, but on August 13, I was the fifth run-away truck to go into the sand pit.

Two other truckers were running with me that night, and after a meal at the Tiny Town Truck Stop atop Mt. Eagle we started descending the mountain. J. P. Cooper and Jim Sutton had lighter loads and started down in front of me. I was grossing around 70,000 pounds. We all had C.B. radios and were constantly in touch with each other. As I started down the mountain, I remember turning on the cab light to check the time. It was almost 11:30 p.m.

I was in ninth gear and that 44,000 pounds plus load began pushing me a little too fast for comfort. J. P. Cooper radioed me to "quit dragging my feet!" I told him my brakes didn't feel right and that I was shifting down to eighth gear. This was sooner than usual with a heavy load. Traffic at the time was very heavy, with both passing lanes full of cars, but my main concern was a slow-moving truck and two cars in front of me. My truck began picking up speed, so I pressed the brake pedal a little harder. Nothing happened!

I radioed Cooper and Sutton that I was in trouble, that my brakes were gone. At this point I pulled both emergency brakes and still nothing happened! I was now against the governor at about 50 or 55 m.p.h. The slow truck and two cars in front of me were now my big worry. I decided to try to down shift into seventh gear. It was a fifty-fifty chance, but if it worked, it would slow me down a little more, putting more distance between me and the slower vehicles in front of me. I knew I had to down shift fast and hard if it worked at all, but it *didn't work!* It was the last chance I had of ever slowing down!

The truck was out of gear, had no brakes, and it was about one-fourth mile to the sand pit. It was free-wheeling and all I could do was hang on and pray. I took a quick look around and traffic on my left was like a wall. Cars behind me had backed off because of smoke boiling from the brake drums.

When I rounded the last curve before the sand pit, the slow truck and two cars passed the entrance to the pit. I radioed Cooper and Sutton I was going into the sand pit.

When I hit the sand, I was shocked by the quickness of the stop. Everything seemed so quiet and all I could hear was the engine idling and crickets singing. It was a most beautiful sound! I couldn't believe I had stopped and I thanked God for being with me and providing a sand pit, seemingly just for me. When a wrecker arrived, the man said I had to be doing at least seventy m.p.h. to go seventy feet into the sand.

Within twenty minutes the highway patrol was on the scene, thanks to a base C.B.-er who heard our predicament and called the patrol office. J. P. Cooper and Jim

Sutton called Nashville for me and were very comforting to me via C.B. radio.

Today, I am alive only because of the grace of God! I thank God for my wife, who at 10:30 p.m. felt that I was in trouble and prayed for my protection. One hour later, I *was* in trouble at the "big cut!" But I had a place of safety to go!

Some reading this story are probably like my runaway truck, and unless you surrender to Christ you have no hope and will soon crash into the rocks below. The sand pit can stop a runaway truck, and that is great, but only God can save a runaway sinner, and that is even greater!

CHAPTER TWENTY-THREE

He Brought Bill Out Of a Deep Pit

by Kathy Bailey

In June of 1971 Bill got a very good paying job with a construction company. We were into "high money" then. Our dates changed from hamburgers to steaks. We were together practically all the time. But that summer was going to change our lives drastically.

On Sunday, June 18, Bill and I went to Sunday school and were persuaded to stay for church by our youth teacher. The conviction of the Lord was so strong in that service that I was not sure what to do. A sister in the Lord came back and invited me to the altar.

I started to go but Bill grabbed my arm and said, "Let's get out of here." So I followed him out.

As we were leaving the church, we decided to go to Fort Worth and eat lunch. We did go to eat and then play Putt Putt. I still remember the game. He won. By that time the conviction I felt had lifted, so we had a fun-filled afternoon.

I worked at that time for a veterinarian. This was a job I got through the school as vocational office education. I started it in my junior year in high school and continued through my senior year.

On Tuesday morning, July 20, 1971, Bill Bailey drove to work late and parked his car crooked because there was not enough time to park it straight. That was the last thing he would remember for several weeks. Just before noon that day his boss thought it looked like rain, so he told Bill and another man to move a piece of plywood to cover the pier holes they were drilling. The problem was that they were unaware that there was already a seventy-three-foot deep pier hole underneath it. Bill took two steps and fell into this pier hole.

Terry was working for the same crew and it took several men to hold him back. This was a terrible ordeal for him.

Finally they found someone to go down by crane to get Bill out. Everyone was sure he was dead. They tied a rope under his arms and managed to get him up about fifteen feet before the rope slipped and Bill hit bottom again. But this time he started moaning, so they knew he was alive. When they successfully pulled him out, they rushed him to St. Paul's Hospital in Dallas where a team of thirteen specialists worked on him. They gave us no hope.

I was devastated. Here was the fun-loving guy I was crazy about in Intensive Care Unit in critical condition. I remembered the times he would act like a motorcycle and do crazy stunts running in the sand at the beach, and here they were talking about amputating his legs below his knees.

He was in a coma and didn't even know I was there. I would go into I.C.U. to tell him I loved him and leave crying. I could only stay five minutes at a time, but I drove a hundred and twenty miles round trip just so I could spend five minutes with the man I loved, Bill Bailey.

Bill's injuries were astounding. He had crushed both feet and ankles, broken his left leg in one place and his right leg in two places, broken his collar bone, crushed the ribs on the right side and collapsed his left lung. Also he had two compression fractures on the back, his jaw was broken in four places and he had a concussion.

When Bill first came out of his coma, he had problems remembering people and places. But God touched him miraculously. Two weeks after his accident and after much prayer and many surgeries, Bill asked everyone to leave because he wanted to talk to me alone. He said, "Kathy, I love you and I want to marry you, but I want you to know I'm going back to church." I was a Methodist and did not understand what he meant at that time, but I agreed.

On Friday, August 13, Bill was released from the hospital just three weeks after his horrible accident. One of his doctors told Bill when he first saw him, "I wouldn't have given a plug nickel for your life but the Lord must want you to live for some reason!"

In September we started to church at the United Pentecostal Church in Cleburne and on September 8, Bill received the Holy Ghost in his wheelchair. On September 11, I received the Spirit. More answered prayer! We were starting our lives over the right way, trusting God for healing and salvation.

The next year was full of ups and downs and many

surgeries. But on July 22, 1972, we were married—one year and two days after the accident.

Life was not at all easy but we were happy. In 1978 Bill worked at Johnson County Sheriff Department as a Crime Scene Investigator. One day as he went with a female deputy to serve some civil papers, they had a car accident. They were hit in the side by an eighteen-wheeler truck. Bill suffered another compression fracture. This was very painful and required a seventeen-day hospital stay.

The Lord was dealing with Bill about the ministry, but he was fighting it. Three months after this accident in a healing line the Lord told the minister preaching that if Bill would accept what God had for him he would completely heal his back. My husband answered with, "Yes Lord, I'll preach Your Word." He has not had any back problems since that night.

To the prom, 1970.

The Bailey Family.

CHAPTER TWENTY-FOUR

Back Surgery—God's Way

By Richard M. Davis

The pain had intensified for two years. From an occasional annoying tingle in my left knee, the pain had increased in frequency and intensity. Something had to be done. Being a person with a high tolerance level for pain, I realized something severe was wrong, for I could no longer bear the pain.

God was my natural source for help. I believed in and preached divine healing and had witnessed its reality on numerous occasions. For some reason, however, God did not choose to heal me immediately. Although I did not understand why God did not heal me, I tried to have faith that God would intervene. Nonetheless, when the pain continued at an intolerable level, I resorted to aspirin and pain relievers to endure the pain. Every four to six hours I would have to take something. Even during the night I would awaken in such pain I could not sleep. Night after night I would arise to take medication.

I was becoming alarmed. The amount of aspirin being consumed could not possibly be healthy. I had not had a restful night for months. My personal life was suffering as well as the areas of my involvement in the ministry. My thinking was not clear and concise. I was fuzzy and lacked concentration. The pain was radiating from the knee into my lower back. It had reached a level of intensity that caused me often to drag my left leg behind me until the medication could take effect.

I began to seek professional medical help. It was several months and physicians later before a definite diagnosis was completed. One doctor had noticed in the X-rays a congenital birth defect in the lower back. He stated that the problem was there to stay and prescribed an anti-inflammatory drug to reduce the pain.

The prescribed medication began to accomplish its task. As long as I stayed on the medicine, my back was fine. The only problem was that nothing was being solved. Only the pain was hidden. I had found temporary relief but was not satisfied. I wanted to be healed.

Even in the absence of my own personal healing, I continued to believe in and preach the divine healing power of God. I did not lose faith in God.

My commitment to Him was, "Lord, if you heal me I will serve You, but if You do not heal me, I will still serve You."

I meant it! I knew that dedication to God had to be without condition or regard to circumstances of life. I knew God loved me and had my best interests at heart. I could still take refuge in Romans 8:28: "And we know that all things work together for good to them that love God, to them who are the called according to his purpose."

Somehow I sensed that God would heal me in His time. I had left my request in the hand of God. It was entirely up to Him. I reached the place where I seldom thought about my problem. I was busy getting on with my life and serving God.

Occasionally I would quit taking my medication or forget to take it with me when I went out of town. Within a few hours, I would be hurting. Within twelve hours the pain would become intolerable, and I would find myself in the same condition as before. I felt like a slave to the medicine—not emotionally, but physically. Without it, I simply could not bear the pain in my back.

After suffering with the problem for two years, I accepted it as a routine of life. Healing was far from my conscious thoughts. Then it happened, suddenly and without warning!

The local church was having a twenty-four hour prayer chain, and I selected 5 o'clock to 6 o'clock in the morning. God always seemed to bless me in a special way in those early morning hours.

The prayer time was going well. Nothing phenomenal was happening, but the presence of God was very near every morning. There were a half dozen or so praying during that particular hour.

One morning toward the end of the week, I was praying on my knees. During the entire week I had not asked for healing one time. I prayed for our missionaries, lost loved ones, and revival around the world. But suddenly a dear saint in prayer began to travail. It was an urgent, wailing spirit of travail.

At that precise moment God knocked me from my knees to my back onto the floor. I continued to pray and worship. I did not know what the dear sister was travailing for, but I knew that God was healing me at that very moment. I just worshiped and thanked God for my healing.

I left the church that morning with a real sense of victory and power. I felt on top of everything. There was only one problem. I was still on medication for my back. If I were healed, how could I know it?

The devil said, "You're not healed. It's the medication that keeps you from hurting. Try putting it aside and see what happens!"

The devil was wrong, and I knew it. God had healed me, and Satan was lying. I responded to Satan accordingly. "Devil, you're a liar! I'm healed."

Still I was afraid to stop the medication. I had tried to stop many times, but in only a few hours I would hurt so badly. I was afraid it might happen again.

I told only my wife of what God had done and privately struggled with Satan on the battlefield of my mind. It was two days before the victory came.

"Lord," I cried, "I'm tired of living under fear. I am going to trust You!"

And with that I laid my medicine aside. I never took another pill from that point forward. Four hours passed, but there was no pain. Six hours went by and still there was victory.

The hours slipped into days, the days turned into weeks. Seven months have passed, and I am free from pain. I can lift up anything I desire. I sleep well at night. The pain has disappeared forever. God healed my back!

The devil has tempted and tried me. For several months the devil fought me with fear when I testified to

God's healing power. I would get restless, tense, and not sleep well, feeling as if my back were trying to hurt.

I responded by testifying even more boldly. I knew what God had done and was determined to give Him the glory, whatever the cost. Now the devil no longer battles me over the matter of my healing. He has given up because God just keeps getting more and more glory. He has found it is not good to stir up the issue.

God answered in His own time, teaching me valuable lessons all the while. He is always right on time and never late. He performed the needed surgery—His way and in His time.

Rev. Richard Davis

CHAPTER TWENTY-FIVE

Back Problems

by Annice Roberts

"Oh," I screamed as I fell on the highly polished hardwood floor of my living room.

"A slipped disc," the first doctor diagnosed. We prayed earnestly but without results. Six different doctors, gave several x-rays and all agreed that indeed I had a slipped disc. I was admitted to the hospital for six days. The doctors then told me they had done all they could for me, and wanted me to go to Nashville, Tennessee, to an orthopedic surgeon.

In Nashville the orthopedic doctor x-rayed me again and said the other doctors were right. "The lowest disc is slipped and another one is nearly slipped," he said. "Your left leg is perishing from the pressure on your sciatic nerve. You need surgery badly! If it was a normal need for surgery I would operate tomorrow, but if I operate you may possibly suffer from this the rest of your life. But if you can endure the pain with the aid of medication

I will wait about the surgery," he advised.

Downhearted, discouraged, depressed, I thought, "I can never do anymore for my family or anyone else. I had rather go on to be with Jesus." Such terrible pain! At times I could hardly endure it.

Early one morning as I lay on my bed praying. The Lord said to me, "If you suffer the rest of your life with this, the stripes were put on My back in vain for you."

Faith began to pour into my heart! Soon pain stopped! I got up and cooked my family's breakfast. From that moment I have not had the first pain from that affliction. That was more then twenty years ago. Praise God! He still answers prayer.

I was examined by two of the doctors later. When I told them of the moment of healing, they both said they believed every word and that it must be wonderful to be touched by a miracle.

CHAPTER TWENTY-SIX

A Canadian Woman's Healing

by Hazel Kaulbach, R.N.

About ten years ago, in 1974, when I began to have problems in my chest, I went to the doctor to have the problem diagnosed. Dr. M. B. Berner, my family doctor in the city of Toronto, Ontario (Canada), sent me for an gastrointestinal series of X-rays. The results showed that I had hiatus hernia with reflux, but it also showed something which in the X-ray looked like a stone. Therefore, the doctor made an appointment for me to go on a Wednesday morning for a gallbladder series.

On the Tuesday night previous to my appointment for the gallbladder series, at prayer meeting I requested prayer. My pastor, Brother Carl Stephenson, and the church had special prayer for me.

On Wednesday I went for the scheduled gallbladder series. The X-rays did not even show my gallbladder, so I was required to go back on Thursday for a repeat of the same X-rays. Once again, the results were negative and showed up nothing, for which I praise God!

Several weeks later I realized that God had also healed the hiatus hernia, for since that time I have had no problems relating to this physical condition. Nor have I had these ten years. I can eat anything at any time with no ill effects.

CHAPTER TWENTY-SEVEN

"I Will Praise. . ."

by Beverly Burk

Trying to condense seven years of blessings and miracles into a few pages is a little like trying to pour a gallon of iced tea into a pint-sized pitcher. My experience with Crohn's Disease was hard and trying, sometimes frustrating and discouraging, yet at the same time encouraging, rewarding and satisfying.

In 1976, a few months after our son Devon Paul was born, I was diagnosed as having granulmatus colitis. It seemed to cause no particular problem, so I saw no reason to change my life-style. My husband Dorsey and I still planned on going to Germany as missionaries as we had since Bible college.

In 1977, we received the long awaited missionary appointment and made plans to live the rest of our lives in the country we loved so much.

I had discussed this change with my doctor, who said that since Germany was very modern I should have no problem living there. Things were in order. I had done all I knew to do and, finally, after years of planning and hoping, dreaming and praying, we were on our way!

During deputation, I started having serious abdominal pains—often severe enough to cause me to double over. This usually occurred about two to three hours after eating and only seemed to be relieved by vomiting and thereby lessening the tightness in my stomach. I thought the extreme pressure a deputational missionary is under was taking its toll on my body and that things would certainly be fine when we got settled in Europe.

The day finally came to say goodbye to our friends in America and hello to our new homeland. It was love at first sight! Germany was much more wonderful than I ever thought possible. Brother and Sister Sam Balca and Brother and Sister Dale Walker did everything they could to make our transition swift and easy. Soon an apartment was found, furniture bought, language school started, Krystin, then six years old, settled in a military school. Life was wonderful—except for my health.

Many days I could not keep anything on my stomach. I had such severe cramps that I would wake my husband groaning in my sleep. I would lie in bed day after day on a heating pad trying somehow to stop the pain. I took very strong pain pills, but nothing seemed to give any relief. When I was able to get up to do a few things, I would often have to hold the wall or furniture. I lost weight until I only weighed ninety-seven pounds. I looked like a skeleton with some skins stretched over it.

The German doctor finally put me in the University Hospital in Wiesbaden for tests. The rooms there had two beds, one chair, one wash basin, two night stands and a crucifix. The showers were down the hall. The entire staff would stop what they were doing to watch this crazy American walk to the showers *every day!* A psychologist was sent for an interview to find why anyone would ask the doctors what they were going to do that day and why. The doctors repeated very painful tests over and over again.

Finally, the wonderful day came when I went home. I was no better, nor had they told me anything about my disease. I was simply sent home without one word. However, I was more than happy to leave any way I could!

Up to this point, I have not mentioned God. There is a basic reason for this rather obvious omission. I had not allowed Him to be involved. *I* was handling this. If the German doctors were correct, if my husband was correct in believing them, if all of this was caused by tension—if I was too intense about life—then all could be cured by relaxing. I really tried to do all that I was told. But I kept going, without asking God for His direct help. I was strong willed and I felt that I could do whatever necessary if I really made up my mind to do it.

Many people tried to help. Brother and Sister Wayne Nigh came often and prayed for me. Brother and Sister William Schmidt came for a seminar and they prayed for me. Many others—whoever came always prayed. However, all the time they prayed, I would be thinking, "God, I could really handle this myself. All You really need to do is show me how to relax."

Soon after I came home from the hospital, a very strange thing happened. For three nights in a row, I dreamed that I was in an airplane, my spirit was very heavy, and somehow I realized that I was taking an emergency leave. Next to me sat a woman in a brown, flowered, silk dress. I didn't understand this at all. My grandmother was in her nineties, but we had already said goodbye to her. I just didn't understand what this was all about.

In May of 1979, my mother called from her hospital room in Portland, Oregon. She had just been told that she had cancer and had only been given six to nine months to live. We had no idea that she was even ill. For days, I went around in shock. Should I go home? Should I wait? What could be done? All during this time I was still extremely weak.

Sometimes there is one incident in your life that changes an entire story. Mine came one day when I had cried until I was too weak to cry any more. I was sitting in the living room—not thinking, not crying—just sitting. I had put some records on the stereo, trying to collect myself. One of Bill Gaither's songs suddenly caught my attention. The words were:

I will praise Him,
Knowing that my praise will cost me everything.
I will praise Him,
Praise Him with the joy that comes from knowing that I have held back nothing.
And He is Lord.
He is Lord.
*HE IS LORD!**

Praise! To praise, not holding back anything at all? Praise knowing that it would cost everything I had? This sounded impossible, but sitting in Wiesbaden, West Germany, on that day in May, I knew somehow I had to learn how.

I sat crying and praying. That day I told God I had no idea how to accomplish this task, but if He would guide me, I would do all I could to learn. I began by thanking Him that I had such terrible nerve problems, that I was a wreck and had made myself that way. Next I thanked Him for my mother's illness, that I had a sixteen-year-old sister that He would have to care for and help grow up, that my father was going to have to try to pastor a church, teach full time in public school, raise Lurissa and still try to stay sane. Needless to say, it didn't sound very thankful, but it was a start.

I'm so grateful that God doesn't expect a perfect job the first time we try something. That day I felt a burden lift and I knew this was the answer I had been looking for.

The next day, I was once again unable to leave my bed, but it was with a different attitude. I thanked God—really thanked Him—and life was good. During that day, I thumbed through the Book of Psalms. I was impressed by the many times that David said, "I will." "I will praise the LORD" (Psalm 7:17). "I will praise thee" (Psalm 9:1). "I will be glad. . .I will sing praise" (Psalm 9:2). Throughout the Psalms it was the same theme: I have problems, *but I will praise.*

Starting to learn to praise by praising for everything seemed a little too difficult, so I started by going one hour, stopping, kneeling, or if I was confined to bed that day, bowing my head and praising God for everything that had happened during the previous hour. Soon I could really praise God *for all that had happened* during that time span. I could praise Him that I had to hold the wall and try to dust. I could praise Him that I could eat two and three bites of supper. I could praise Him that the two and three bites of supper had not stayed down.

Praise changed everything. I became happy, almost excited. Even when I was very sick, I still could learn to look for things to praise for. It became an all-consuming task.

One day I was extremely weak. Several people had told me how terrible I looked and I really needed to gain some weight. I knew that, but I also knew that I could not keep anything down long enough to get any nutritional value from it. I started reading the Bible to receive some encouragement from somewhere.

I opened to Psalm 41.

> *"Blessed is he that considereth the poor: the LORD will deliver him in time of trouble. The LORD will preserve him, and keep him alive; and he shall be blessed upon the earth: and thou wilt not deliver him unto the will of his enemies. The LORD will strengthen him upon the bed of languishing. . .An evil disease, say they, cleaveth fast unto him; and now he that lieth he shall rise up no more."*

I couldn't believe what I was reading! It sounded like David had been with me the last few days! But David had said if I had considered the poor (which I knew I had) that He would preserve me. That chapter became the fort I would run to. Whenever I felt discouraged or someone had made me feel depressed, I would read that chapter and feel comforted and promised.

Romans 8:28 also changed me. I had read and memorized this verse as a child. I had read and memorized it as a teenager. I had read and memorized it as a young adult, but when I started to praise God for it, I learned how to use it. I thanked God that whatever this disease was and involved in, it was for my good. I really started to appreciate the lessons I was learning from it.

I started looking at this affliction as a "post graduate" course in Christian Living. I was determined to get an A—or at least pass. I sure did not want to have to take it again!

Summer and fall came and went and I continued to learn to praise. By constantly working on it, praise became a continual attitude. I could smile and really be joyful even when I hurt. I could be thankful even when I could not get out of bed. I could praise when I could not keep food down. The circumstances had not changed a bit. I still woke my husband up groaning at night. The pain was still terrible. But *I* had changed!

Christmas in Germany was so much fun! But I could not get away from the feeling that I had better keep things done up. I did laundry every day or two. One night I had the dream about the airplane again and told my husband, "Let's get everything ready. I'm going to have to go to the States soon."

We checked airline schedules. A church in the States had told us that if we needed anything to let them know. (It's dangerous to tell missionaries that!) We called and the pastor was wonderful. Yes, he had meant what he had offered and he would be glad to help.

The first week in January, my father called from

Portland. The doctors there had done surgery on Mom and had given her just a few days to live. If I wanted to see her alive, I'd better come home right away.

Thank God, He was in control. Everything was ready. I simply packed the suitcases and got on the plane. As I sat there, I happened to look at the lady on my left. She was wearing a brown, flowered, silk dress. God never allows anything to come our way that He hasn't prepared us for!

When I got to the States, everyone seemed thrilled—and except for the comments about my lack of weight, it was good to see everyone.

Life established a routine. I would be at the hospital after Dad and Lurissa left for school. Many people wanted to see Mom, so I tried to help the nurses by ushering people in and out, trying to keep Mom from getting too tired and uncomfortable. After school Dad would come and I would leave for a while. Lurissa and I would go up after supper and stay for most of the evening. There was no time to stay in bed and, with God's help, I didn't need to miss a day. If Mom had known how sick I was, she'd have thrown a fit—dying and not dying! I knew my mom!

On January 29, 1980, my mother went on. Her last words were, "Oh, what a beautiful light!" Because I had learned to praise, her death didn't devastate me. Death in the Christian home can be a victorious experience.

After Mom's funeral, my aunt, my sister-in-law, and I tried to get things organized for Dad and Lurissa. The house had to be gone over. Boxes of things my mother had saved had to be gone through. Her personal items had to be disposed of. And all this time, I knew I was getting weaker. Towards the end of the job, my aunt and

Miriam, my sister-in-law, had to do most of it. I just could not seem to get it done.

Finally, things were as settled as the three of us could make them and I felt it was time to go home to Europe. By now I could barely get through the day without going to bed, but I felt that if I could just get home and rest, I'd be fine. I really missed my children and my husband and I wanted to go home.

I was scheduled to leave at 8:00 on Thursday morning, so before Bible study on Wednesday night, I laid my clothes that I had decided to wear in the order I would be putting them on. I didn't want to waste one minute going home.

During church, I really felt sick and weak and spent most of the service in the church restroom. On the way home that night, Dad talked me into going to the hospital for some pain pills to help me get back to Germany. After an X-ray, I was told an intestinal blockage had been found and I would have to be admitted.

It was hard to praise that night. I missed Dorsey and the children so much, but it felt good to get a shot and have some relief from the pain.

A day or two after admittance, a specialist came to tell me I had what was called Crohn's Disease—that there was no cure and it would plague me all of my life. An immediate operation was necessary to remove the blockage.

Things were happening too quickly for me to think. A few days after I had planned to be home, I had surgery in which the doctors removed three feet of small intestine.

Soon after the operation, I felt strong enough to wonder about this strange disease. After questioning, I found that Crohn's Disease creates small nodules or masses of inflamed tissue that penetrates into the wall of the intestinal tract. It often skips around in the bowel, so it cannot be cured by surgery.

The medical world doesn't know why it strikes young people between eighteen and twenty-five years old; they don't understand why it's more prevalent in the city than rural areas or why it has increased 200% in the last ten years. They have no cure, nor do they know the cause.

One doctor later told me that when he tells someone he has Crohn's Disease, he is sentencing a young person to a lifetime of pain and suffering from which there is no escape. Then he made a statement which told me the seriousness of this disease; "I would rather tell someone that they have cancer instead of Crohn's. At least with cancer, they will usually die."

One doctor told me that if I had not had surgery that within six months the build up behind the blockage would have caused my intestines to rupture, after which I would have had about twenty-four hours to live.

"Would the pain have been any worse?" I asked. "No," was the answer. Then I realized that I had not had six months to live, but eight hours. If I had gotten on the plane, I may have died. I spent a long time thanking God for His mercy.

It seemed the time in the hospital was a time of drawing closer to God. About 5:00 a. m. every day we communed, and these moments can be described only as sweet. One morning I awoke thinking of Psalm 121:1: "I will lift up mine eyes unto the hills, from whence cometh my help." David was talking not only about physical mountains, but also about life's trials and experiences. Often we can look back at things we have had victory over and receive strength to face our next challenge. I decided I would never have a trial—without putting another mountain in "my" mountain range!

There were many setbacks—blood transfusions, this wasn't going right, something else wasn't right. Finally Dorsey decided he'd better come—and was I ready to see him!

My health improved and, three months after I left the hospital I returned home to Europe. I was feeling great and ready to do our part for revival in Europe.

My husband and I had a burden for the city of Munich, so we went down on a fact-finding trip. Only once before in my life had I ever felt so completely at home from the minute of arrival, and that was in Kingston, Jamaica. The experience re-occurred in Munich. I wanted to throw my arms wide and shout, "I'm home!" And as I looked at the sin, the sex shops, the empty faces, and the locked doors to the many high-rise apartments, my heart tore. We made plans for a move.

My husband had gone to Munich with the truck and the children and I followed later in our SFC car. I was enjoying the fact that there was no speed limit on the autobahn when construction narrowed the road. The car on my right jerked into my lane and, out of reflex action, I twisted the wheel away from it, putting my car in the oncoming lane. At speeds of 80-85 mph, there seemed no way to avoid death, but at the moment I felt the warmth of Someone's hands over mine. The car immediately straightened—in the correct lane. At the next rest stop, Krystin, Devon, and I had ourselves a praise service!

Munich was wonderful! I enrolled in a new language school. We started to make contacts. I was feeling good.

It looked like the battle was won.

In the midst of this good time, I told God I wanted a meek and quiet spirit. (See I Peter 3:4.) Not long after my prayer, I became ill again. Eventually my health became so poor that Dorsey called Brother Scism for advice. A month to the day after we had dedicated our chapel in a glorious service, much like Solomon must have experienced at the dedication of the Temple, it was decided that we should return to the States on emergency medical furlough.

I really don't remember much about packing. I remember being in tremendous pain. I remember God supplying the help I needed. Sister Carol Rash and her daughter Darla came over from Vienna; LaVonne Pugh, whose husband was stationed in Munich, came out; and Jeanne Collins came from Inzlingen to help. Brother Collins and Brother Goodwin came to help Dorsey load the truck with the furniture to be stored in Wiesbaden.

We spent the night before leaving at the home of Brother and Sister John Goodwin. Everyone except me went on to service. I walked the floor wondering how I could ever make a sixteen-hour-plane-ride with two small children. At 9:00, I suddenly got relief. It was instantaneous and I didn't ask why. I simply thanked God.

We flew into San Francisco and later went to the church in El Sobrante, pastored by Brother B. J. Robison. An elderly sister walked up and asked what had happened to me on Wednesday at 2:00 a.m. She said she had been awakened with a tremendous burden and had spent those early hours interceding for me. Two a.m. Pacific Standard Time was 9:00 p.m. in Germany. God was still controlling things!

After the medical examinations in Portland, Oregon, it was decided that I should be given a colostomy. This surgical procedure involves re-routing the intestine to end at an opening (an ostomy) in the abdominal wall and bypassing the rectum.

I opposed this surgery with all I had. *No way* would I wear a bag to catch the waste. NO WAY!

At this same time, the Foreign Missions Board wisely decided not to reappoint us to Germany. Until my health was better, Dorsey needed to stay close to me and not travel all over the country on deputation. I loved Germany. I loved the people and felt sick about not returning. But it really felt wonderful to know that my disease would be treated here in the States. We knew the Board's decision was in the will of God.

Although we experienced great relief over not going back to Europe until my health improved, we did not know what we were to do next. The next ten months were a struggle.

In October, I decided the quality of life I was enduring could not be worse than living with a colostomy. I could not go anywhere unless a bathroom was near—many shopping malls included! So in early November I had the necessary surgery. Two weeks later, I had another surgery to remove yet another intestinal blockage.

After the first surgery I was told the doctors had planned to remove the rectal stump, thus making the colostomy permanent. But due to tremendous inflammation, they had decided to wait. During the second surgery, they saw such improvement that it was again decided not to remove that area. They did not understand what was happening, but I did. God had promised complete healing!

In December, Brother Harry Scism called my hospital room to talk to Dorsey. The Foreign Missions workload at World Evangelism Center had grown to the point that they needed someone to help, primarily in the area of publications—promotional items such as the *Global Witness* and training materials for use in the foreign Bible schools. Would Dorsey be interested? There was much rejoicing that day! God was giving us another area of Foreign Missions to serve in!

After our move back to St. Louis, my health became worse and then tolerable—only to revert to worse. Back and forth. In the hospital for tests. Out for a few weeks. Back in for more tests. In one year I was in the hospital seven times! I knew there was a blockage, but the tests did not show it.

During the winter of 1983, I was reading my Bible and the words of Isaiah 30:19-21 seemed to stand literally away from the Bible. I knew my experience with Crohn's was almost over.

In March, 1983, my doctor came running into my hospital room. The blockage had been found. Surgery was quickly scheduled and in the pre-operative discussion, Doctor Berwald mentioned he would probably take out the rectal stump.

The first thing I remember after surgery was seeing my husband beside my bed having a terrible time sitting still. As soon as he saw I was awake, he said, "They can't find any Crohn's!"

"That's nice," I replied and went back to sleep.

As soon as I really awoke, I immediately remembered what Dorsey had said! There was no visible Crohn's!

The next day the doctor told me that there had been

a blockage caused by a slipped staple from a previous operation. Then he said the words I'd been waiting to hear for so long: "We can't find any Crohn's." I started crying and asked him to repeat himself and please just one time—please say it!

When was I healed? I don't know—possibly when Brother Jack Yonts and Brother C. M. Becton stopped work to come to my home and anoint me. Or it could have been one of the many times that Pastor Guy Roam prayed for me. Or possibly it was some saint somewhere around the world who had touched God's throne in my behalf. I don't know when the work was done, but I have not been hospitalized in two years—an impossibility in my former condition.

While sitting and thinking about the last seven years, I realized something often overlooked. God can speak a body in or out of existence. This is not a great thing for Him. But God cannot change an attitude or a spirit. He can provide the climate, but the willingness to change has to generate from a submissive and contrite Christian.

One night I became discouraged because of some problems with my colostomy that have developed since deciding to write this article. I asked God for a verse of Scripture and Philippians 1:6 immediately came to mind: "Being confident of this very thing, he which hath begun a good work in you will perform it until the day of Jesus Christ."

On four separate occasions, one of the goals of surgery has been to remove the rectal area. Each time, for a different reason, it was not done. After the last surgery, the doctor admitted he was not sure why it was not done. But I do. The colostomy will be reversed. God has promised and it will happen.

The disease of Crohn's has been a positive one. I have learned how to praise. I have learned more about faith. In fact, I have developed my own definition of faith: Faith is ability to relax in adverse circumstances, *knowing* they are for your good.

I don't know what the future holds, but with God's help, I will continue to raise my hands and sing, "I will praise Him. . . ."

* *Used by permission of Gaither Music Co.*

At the start of Bev's sickness, December 1978.

Bev Burk, German driver's license January 1980.

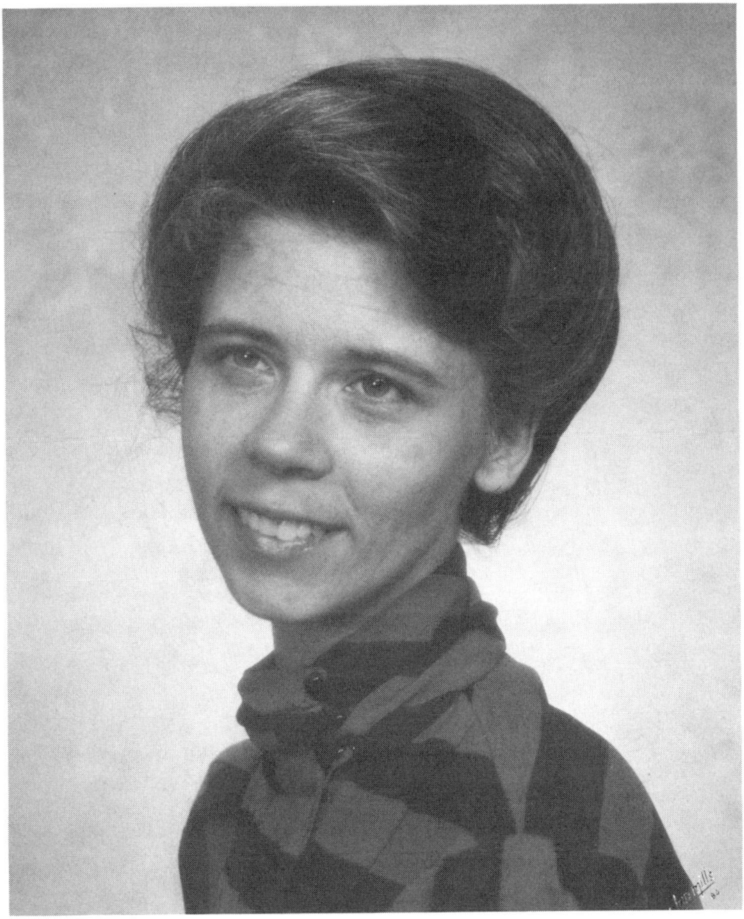

Bev Burk, 1984.

CHAPTER TWENTY-EIGHT

Three Miracles

by O. C. Marler

The Child Healed

One afternoon I was called by an elderly lady. She asked, "Brother Marler, would you go to the hospital and pray for a little six-year-old girl who has leukemia? She has already been given four pints of blood, and is not expected to live much longer." Inquiring about their religious persuasion, I found that there was no trace of Pentecostal belief in their background.

Feeling the urgency of the situation, I went to the hospital without delay. I could not shake the awkwardness that I always feel when I face this type of thing. I parked with extreme care. Each step I took down that long hospital corridor felt like a clap of thunder in my ears. As I approached the door of the child's room, I noticed that I was on tiptoe.

Inside the room the environment was tense, and I hoped the elusive feeling I was reaching for was the substance of hope, "faith." "I'm Brother Marler," I said, quickly looking around at those in the room. "Her grandmother asked me to come and pray." I was drawn to a beautiful little blond girl who was sitting up in the bed, a smile on her face. Her parents were extremely cordial.

"Do you know anything at all about divine healing?" I asked.

Both parents shook their head negatively, "No, sir, I don't believe we do." Then I explained to them James 5:14, which instructs us as believers to call for the elders of the church if we are sick. The elders will then anoint the sick person with oil in the name of the Lord and pray, whereby the prayer of faith will save the sick person and heal him.

"Reverend Marler, whatever you normally do to enact this, we would be happy for you to do it now," the child's father responded.

I had never had it put on me in just that way, and I felt the force of being nothing but a human being. However, I knew what God could do. Simply stepping over to the bed, I took a small bottle of oil out of my coat pocket. "See this? I am going to put some of this oil on my finger and then I'll put it on your head. I don't want you to be afraid. I'm going to pray to Jesus and ask Him to heal you."

The child smiled and nodded at me. She did not seem afraid.

Being very conscious of the decree that I had made, and also of the fact that this was a new experience for this family, I thought, "Oh God, I wish I could pray a sophisticated and elegant sounding prayer." But all I could think of to say was, "In the name of the Lord Jesus, I ask you to heal this little girl."

I would like to be able to say that the windows rattled and the lightning crashed, but it didn't happen that way. I was almost blushing with embarrassment. The family was still cordial. I left the room. . .still human. Driving home, I felt as if the whole human race was looking at me grinning and mocking. Even in the safety of my home I felt exposed.

After about two hours the phone rang. As soon as I answered I felt the excitement of the grandmother. "Oh! Reverend Marler! The doctor came in right after you left. He made his routine examinations and told the nurses to stop all medication. He said something miraculous had taken place, and evidently there was something in the blood she was given that counteracted those wild blood cells." Grandmother was so excited that she could hardly talk. Her words stumbled over each other. "And Brother Marler, do you know what else they said? They said, 'This blood came from Wadley's blood bank. We're going to trace back and see who the donors are. We have probably made a great medical breakthrough.' "

"Hold everything!" I interrupted. "If you're going to trace that blood, you'll have to go all the way back to Calvary's cross. And Grandma, I promise you if you get one drop of it, there will be enough healing power in it that everyone in this hospital can get up and walk out single file."

When I hung up the phone the impact of what our Lord's blood can do was about to explode inside me. I realized that to fully comprehend this reality would be impossible.

I am still awkward and helpless when faced with situations like this. Polished prayers and dramatic settings have never influenced Jesus favorably, but He gives His kingdom to a child with quiet faith.

The Gift of An Organ

I sipped a comfortable cup of coffee, and revelled in the morning sun that beamed warmly into my home in Dallas. It felt good to look out the window this morning and think back over the past few months. I was flooded with the realization that we had our new building completed. We had built a new church from scratch.

Accompanied by anticipation, anxiety, and loneliness, my family and I had moved to Dallas. We knew no one; however, before long we acquired land, built a building, and gathered in a congregation. A revival with Brother and Sister Kenneth Phillips was scheduled to begin soon.

Since Sister Phillips is quite an accomplished organist, I desperately wanted an organ in the church. I felt excitement and optimism rise in me as I showered and dressed and drove over to Garland, Texas, to one of the largest stores in the area that sold pianos and organs. I approached a salesman and asked about renting an organ.

"Sir, would you consider buying one?" he queried. "We don't rent, but I think we could work comfortably with you on some sort of credit arrangement."

"Oh no. We are not able to do anything at the present but rent," I replied.

With a studied look he said, "Just one moment. Let me go check." He disappeared into the back of the store toward some offices. I calmly amused myself by picking the best looking organ on the floor and getting a mental picture of Sister Phillips sitting there playing. With my hand I even wiped a little dust off the smooth surface. Then standing in front of the show window with my hands in my pockets, I soaked up some warm sun.

Before long the man came back and asked, "Reverend, what would you say if I just gave your church an organ?"

"Why, sir, I'd be the biggest fool in Dallas, Texas, if I didn't accept it!" I quickly responded.

"Do you want one out of the crate, or do you want one off the floor?" He asked politely.

I decided since he was being so benevolent, he should make the decision. That very afternoon a new organ was delivered to our church. Across the invoice, which I still have in my files, was marked "donation."

At a later date a fellow minister was talking to the store owner who had donated the organ to us. He casually said, "I surely appreciate your donating the organ to Reverend Marler's church."

With strong feeling, the man said, "Sit down. I want to tell you the story about that. It was a morning just like any other. I was sitting at my desk looking out my office window when the strangest thing happened to me. It was stranger than anything that has ever happened in my life. I saw Brother Marler walking to the store, and something told me 'Whatever that man asks you for, give it to him.' " Tears were spilling down his cheeks before he finished telling the story to my friend.

That clear sunny morning in Dallas was one of the greatest mornings of my life, not because of the monetary value, but to know that God was still in the miracle-working business, and that He would work through me.

God Visited The Intensive Care Unit

Thoughts of a quiet evening colored by a mauve and gold sunset slipped into the unoccupied areas of my mind as I drove into my driveway one evening in Dallas. However, I had not been home very long that evening before I received a shattering phone call that is all too familiar in a pastor's home. A man had attempted suicide in his back yard. He was not in the church, but his wife and daughter were. "Will you come immediately?"

I gathered from the phone conversation that he went to the back yard, and with a gun, aimed at his heart but missed. His arm was nearly severed. I advised the girls not to go into the back yard, and assured them that I would be there soon.

While a stricken family paced inside a house, ambulance lights slashed through the dusk, and a squad of medics moved silently into the back yard and quickly put their burden on a stretcher. The man was taken to Parkland Hospital, the same hospital where President Kennedy was taken.

I stayed at the hospital with the family most of the night. They were pressured with making the decision as to whether or not to amputate the arm. They decided to amputate. The man was in excruciating pain, which nothing could dull.

Finally, early in the morning hours, the family asked me to go into the intensive care unit and pray for him. Later he testified that the pain left instantly, when I prayed and he said he never had another pain in the arm area from that day forward. His fever also went down.

The miracles didn't stop that morning with one man.

After getting a little rest and refreshing myself from the strenuous night at the hospital, I went back to the waiting room where a group of people were sitting. I heard someone say, "Here comes the preacher." They stopped me and someone said, "Reverend, we've heard what happened in the intensive care unit. All of us have someone in the unit, and we'd like for you to pray for our folks."

I got permission to go into the intensive care unit. Of course, I couldn't keep it straight who was who, but I prayed for everyone there. Everyone in the intensive care unit was healed that afternoon.

There is no glory in that for me. I could not heal one of them. I felt so helpless and on the spot, but if God be for us, who can be against us, and there is wonderful glorious power in His name. I love Dallas, Texas, as much as I ever did, even though I don't live there any more. When I look back I find myself rejoicing, not because of material things. . .money, buildings, land. . .but I'm thinking fondly of some mountaintops with the Lord. . .some times when He increased and I decreased.

Rev. O. C. Marler

CHAPTER TWENTY-NINE

We Have Learned To Trust Him

by Ann Brinkley Luther

The year of 1970 was entered into by two very excited and happy people. My husband and I had been married four years and were just two years into our first pastorate. We were expecting our first child. Both of our families were healthy and well, and we were looking forward to a great year.

Prior to 1970 I had worked for the Department of Human Services of Tennessee for seven years and my husband had taught high school in our home town of Bemis, Tennessee. We had both had very happy and secure lives, with basically no sicknesses or real problems to speak of. Since children we had both been very active in our local church and loved our Lord above all else. Our desire had been to serve the Lord and we were very happy that we were now in full-time gospel work and could devote all of our energies into the ministry.

On Monday morning, June 22, after having completed a week of Junior Youth Camp work and entertaining two young ministers, Rick Flowers and Mike Yarbro, over the weekend, I checked into the Maury County Hospital in Columbia, Tennessee, for the long awaited birth of our child. Both sets of parents were called in and many of our church people came to wait out what they thought was going to be the final hours of labor. Check-in time was 12:00 noon. Our parents arrived around 3:00 p.m. and church people began to gather in the waiting room about 7:00 p.m.

At 3:00 a.m. the next morning, the doctor returned to the waiting room to inform its weary and anxious occupants that complications had occurred and that both my life and the life of the child were in danger. Immediate and desperate prayer was made then and there. We thank the Lord for His intervention and where it had been thought that one or both of us would die, a healthy, normal baby boy was born on June 23 at 3:14 p.m. by Caesarean section. That baby boy is today a handsome, normal, and intelligent fourteen-year-old, even though the doctor was concerned at the time because of the length of time the baby was in the birth canal. We feel that everything went well because that night in the waiting room and in homes throughout the small town of Hohenwald, earnest prayer was made.

The weeks following our child's birth were busy ones. There were the Regional Bible Quiz Tournaments in Birmingham, Alabama, and a two-week revival with David and Rick Flowers. The days were busy and my husband failed to mention to me that he had found a lump that he felt needed medical attention. An appointment was made with the family physician on a date after his return from General Conference in Portland, Oregon. His physician advised him to see a urologist for further examination. An appointment was made with Dr. James Roy Appleton of Jackson, Tennessee, for Wednesday, August 26.

I was awakened in the early morning hours of that unforgettable Wednesday by the groaning and travailing prayers of my husband coming from the living room. I had not even been concerned about the doctor's appointment up until that point and had felt that it would just be a quick visit to the doctor's office, a prescription to be filled, and no more. My husband had not been worried or concerned either until he was awakened by the prompting of the Lord in those early morning hours to pray. Later that same day I would go back in my thoughts to those prayers and take comfort in them. I felt that was definitely an instance of the Spirit making intercession for us.

My husband had someone appointed to take care of the Bible study that night and we took our eight-week-old son and drove seventy-five miles to Jackson, Tennessee, for his 11:00 appointment. After leaving David with his grandparents, we rushed to the clinic to be on time for the appointment. We were relieved to have the day away from our responsibilities and had planned lunch and a shopping trip afterwards. To pass the time while Bill was with the doctor, I sat down beside a man that we had both known and gone to church with for many years. In a short time his wife came out of the doctor's office with the joyful news that she had been declared cured of cancer after five years.

As we were all three rejoicing over her good news, Bill emerged from the office with a very sober expression. Taking me by the arm, he hurriedly walked me to the car, explaining on the way that he needed to be admitted to the hospital. As we drove out of the parking lot he explained that the doctor had told him, "Bill, you have a tumor and when I say tumor, I mean cancer."

I could not put words on this page that would explain our feelings at that point. We felt numb. I remember thinking that I should be crying, or screaming, or doing something other than just sitting there clutching the baby's shoes which I had brought along to use as a measure for a new pair. Calmly we tried to reassure each other as we drove straight to my parents' house where we could be alone to pull our thoughts together and pray. Our church was called, plans were made for the baby, and we were checked into the hospital by 1:00 p.m.

Word spread around to the surrounding churches quite rapidly and before Bill was wheeled into surgery at 2:00 p.m., there were seven United Pentecostal Church ministers standing around his hospital bed praying for him. At 4:00 p.m. we were back in the room listening to the doctor give us the diagnosis of "Seminoma-Embryonal Carcinoma." The doctor outlined for us what he thought would be the best form of treatment and left the family in stunned silence to regroup our emotions and then to plan for our baby and church for the next few days.

As late afternoon waned into night, friends and family departed to their own homes. Bill and I were left alone to talk over the events of this most memorable day of our lives.

After lights had been dimmed and final medications given for the evening, we were thankful to see Jean and Raymond Hensley walk through the doors. After church these folks had driven from Hohenwald to bring greetings and prayers from the saints there. This was just what the young pastor had needed, because after they left, he settled down into a deep, peaceful sleep for the remainder of the night.

When his slow, steady breathing assured me that he was fast asleep, I quietly tiptoed into the hallway. There, leaning against the wall which was bathed in the soft light from the Intensive Care Unit directly across the way, I wept quietly the tears that had been held back throughout the busy day. The next thing I felt was an arm around my shoulder and a voice tenderly quoting Scripture to me and giving words of encouragement. After several minutes of talking with the nurse, I went back to my chair to sleep, and the nurse disappeared through the doors leading to ICU.

In the weeks and months that followed, I could never find the nurse to thank her for her help to me, but I do thank the Lord that He sent comfort to me that lonely night.

After a six-day stay in the hospital for the removal of the tumor, we moved in with his parents so that Bill could begin radiation treatments. Those days were filled with daily trips to the hospital for his intensive cobalt therapy which was followed by several bouts of vomiting daily. We always looked forward to the weekends and holidays because the X-ray department would be closed, and we would have one whole day free of nausea.

Bill existed for almost five weeks on boiled custard and soup. His weight loss dropped to 145 pounds from 195 pounds, and his complexion turned a light yellow color. The lower back and abdomen turned black from the burning of the radiation.

We were allowed to return to our faithful church and home for a few weeks the latter part of September. During all of this time, our church people in Hohenwald drove the seventy-five miles to visit their ailing young pastor and leave their prayers and offerings with us. The radiation treatments were not covered by the insurance, but with offerings from church people, friends and relatives, we were able to pay the full amount in cash and leave the hospital with less than an $80.00 debt.

On Sunday, October 18, District Superintendent, Reverend W. M. Greer came to Hohenwald and dedicated our baby in a lovely service which had been postponed due to Bill's illness. After lunch we drove back to Jackson where Bill entered the hospital for a radical retroperitoneal lymphadenectomy and appendectomy. After the admission was accomplished and supper was eaten, we were allowed to get a pass and attend church that night at the Bemis Pentecostal Church.

The next morning before I arrived at the hospital to visit, the doctor made his rounds and talked with my husband. In response to Bill's questioning about what Doctor Appleton expected to find during the operation, his reply was this: "Bill, we could find absolutely nothing, and then again, this cancer could have spread. This is why we are doing the surgery. We want to find out."

When I entered the room I could sense the despondency in my husband's spirit. We were both dreading, of course, the impending pain and suffering we knew he would suffer from the surgery but of far greater weight to him was the worry and concern for me and the baby. Just two months prior to this time, we had cancelled a very expensive life insurance policy that we had bought when we were both working.

He told me what the doctor had said and, taking me by the hand, he pulled me down to sit on the bed beside him. In a voice heavy with desperation he said, "Honey, we have got to have victory today over this fear. Let's pray." During the prayer, he turned his face to the wall and began to weep. He testified later that during that prayer, the fear left to be replaced by peace and assurance that all would be well.

Upon leaving the hospital I had to go by the drug store and pick up a few items including formula to make up for the baby. As I emerged into the afternoon sunlight, for no apparent reason, the floodgates of emotions that I had kept under close wrap for the last two months emptied out a torrent of tears. I ran to my car and sat there trying to bring myself under control. I started the car and attempted to drive but could not see for the tears, so I just stopped in the middle of the parking lot and laid my head on the wheel.

I turned my head at the sound of someone pecking on the window and found Pastor Claude Fields standing beside my car. I opened the door and he knelt there beside the car and talked and prayed with me. He said that he just happened to be passing by on the highway and saw my car on the crowded parking lot. I believe the Lord sent him to me at that particular time of need.

The next morning Bill was wheeled into surgery at 7:30. The anesthetic was started at 8:05 and the surgery itself was begun at 8:22 and lasted until 11:35. Although a radical node dissection was made along the aorta, all nodes were found to be negative. All vital organs, including the lungs, heart, stomach, kidneys, bladder and intestines, were checked for any evidence of metastatic disease. The incision was so extensive and tissue had been so damaged by radiation treatment that it was necessary to use wire retention sutures which proved to be extremely painful during the healing process. Bill spent four days in ICU and fourteen more days in the hospital.

During that time of stay in the hospital we were overwhelmed by the loving support in prayer, money and visits that was given to us by people throughout the length and breadth of this nation. We shall never forget the lessons learned during those trying days. We learned how important just a word, or a card, or phone call can mean in times of trouble. People who care are much more precious than silver and gold.

We were overjoyed when on Wednesday, November 25, we were able to gather our belongings together and return to our home in Hohenwald. It was indeed a happy Thanksgiving Eve for our family. We arrived just in time to attend the Community Thanksgiving Service. All of the pastors of other denominations had taken an offering for us and had been requesting prayer in their local churches. We thank the Lord for their concern and assistance and it was truly a Community Thanksgiving Service that night. My husband was able on December 11 to again step to the pulpit in the Hohenwald United Pentecostal Church and preach in the service. He preached that day on "The Will of God" from Mark 3:31-35.

There are some who are of the opinion that "divine healing" can only be claimed when a doctor is not consulted or used. I disagree with that premise. All healing that is asked for in Jesus' name is supernatural, whether it be instantaneous or progressive. It is "divine" because it came from Him.

I can see the hand of the Lord throughout my husband's sickness. I feel we were directed to the best doctor in his field of medicine, and he was a man of prayer. In fact, one of the physicians assisting in the surgery has since been Spirit-filled. Our physician was a man who believed in prayer. He told us following Bill's surgery that he had done all he could do, now his healing or recovery would have to be in the hands of the Lord. We saw God's provision in my unknown nightime visitor in the hospital corridor, in the granting of peace to Bill the day before surgery, in Pastor Fields finding me in all the hundreds of people in the shopping center parking lot, in Bill's recovery, and in so many more instances that time would not allow us to tell in this one chapter. We can only say, "Thank God for the miracles that added such a dimension to our attitudes and emotions and that caused us to realize our own mortality in our youth. It has added more appreciation for every other day of the rest of our lives."

In the ensuing years. Bill has made yearly visits to Dr. Appleton for extensive tests which have all proven to be negative. Every August has been a time of thankful celebration for our family as we remember what God has done for us. In more recent days God has revealed Himself in a miraculous way in our family again as He has intervened in a marvelous healing of my eyes.

All of my life I have been an avid reader, consuming all types of reading materials. Together, my husband and I have accumulated a large library which has been a source of help and pleasure to us as well as our family and friends.

It has been a joy through the years to read to my children. My bedside table has always been occupied by current reading materials as well as those books and articles I anticipated reading in the future. Without noticing it, my reading began tapering off, book stores were not visited as frequently, and my children, especially my youngest son, would have to ask me to read or share some interesting story or book with them.

After about a year and a half I began to notice that I would have black "floaters" in front of my vision and a great deal of visual distortion. Depth perception was very poor and I could not read a line in the newspaper or a book without running my finger along under the words to stay on the same line. I realized at this point that I needed something other than just a routine visit for my glasses to be changed.

I made an appointment with a local ophthalmologist. After completing the routine examination, he requested that it was urgent that I stay that day for a special test that was needed. Although he would not venture to make a diagnosis without the results of the test, he did reveal to me, after my direct questioning, that I had a problem which he felt could eventually cause total blindness.

Upon our return from the 1984 General Conference of the United Pentecostal Church in Anaheim, an appointment was made to learn the results of the eye test. As we looked at the X-rays, the doctor pointed to a small spot which was located very near to the center of my field of vision. He stated that I had a degenerative condition of the retina that was rare in a person my age, but was common to a person in their 80's or 90's. With this particular condition, the retina would continue to thin and as it did so, cracks would occur and fill with fluid which would result in a loss of vision. If one of these cracks occurred in the center of my field of vision, which this first one almost did, it would immediately cause blindness. He felt that this first crack was so near the center of my vision that it was inoperable and he was sending me to Memphis, Tennessee, to a specialist of world renown reputation for a second opinion.

In the intervening days before my appointment in Memphis, my thoughts and emotions would swing between denial of what I had been told by the doctor and a great overwhelming fear that I would wake up one morning to total or partial blindness. In talking with friends and acquaintances, I would always request prayer. However, upon my visit to Memphis all of my denials had to bow to reality as this man of medicine concurred with the first diagnosis. He decided to do the surgery anyway as there was nothing to lose with trying. He felt there was no time to lose, so surgery was done within the next two hours. He told me that even if the surgery was successful in sealing the cracked retina, that I could not and would not regain the vision that I had already lost in the eye.

After surgery I was sent home to wait a month before returning for a check-up. When the patch was taken from my eye after returning home, it was difficult for me to drive and impossible to read or write.

A week and a half after surgery my family and I attended a service where my husband Reverend Bill Luther, Reverend Mike Tuminello and Sister Vesta Mangun anointed me with oil and prayed for me. The power and presence of God came down and touched me that night. I believe I left that service with the work of healing in my body. A few days later, Reverend and Mrs. Gayln Allen stood in our living room and together we prayed for healing for my eyes. Again, God in a very definite and mighty way touched my body. During this time, fasting and prayer was made by our local church members at the Bemis Pentecostal Church, and other friends and churches throughout the nation. A dear friend, Sister Sue Nix, missionary to Costa Rica, sent a note to me saying that she was setting aside a day of fasting and prayer for my complete healing. Friends and contacts such as these are far more valuable and precious than gold. My husband and Sister Thetus Tenney were especially supportive during this time and I will always be grateful for their encouragement and interest.

Upon my return to Memphis on December 4, 1984, the doctor's first words when he looked into my eyes were "unbelievable," "amazing." He then told me that when he began the surgery he had found more involvement than he had expected and therefore he had to hit my field of vision dead center with the laser and was surprised that I could see at all. What was more amazing was the fact that with my glasses on I had 20/30 + 1 vision in the eye. With three more months of natural healing process in the eye, he was expecting even that vision to improve. If that is true, I will eventually end up with better vision in the eye than when this ordeal began. Every day I can notice an improvement and I thank God for it.

My husband asked me to give my testimony to the church on the following Sunday morning. However, on Saturday morning at 4:30 a.m. I awoke to an excruciating headache which lasted all that day and throughout the night. I awoke Sunday morning with the same pain. As we sat at breakfast I told my husband that I would not be able to teach my class or even go to church that morning because of the severe pain. At that very moment the telephone rang and our Sunday school superintendent asked me if I could combine my class with another class and teach both of them that morning. Rather than tell him that I could not be there, I said that I would be glad to teach both classes. As I left the table and began to dress for Sunday school, the severe pain that had plagued me for the last twenty-eight hours left completely and I went to church that morning with two miraculous testimonies of healing instead of one.

Many, many mornings following my surgery, before I would ever put my feet on the floor to get up, I would remind the Lord that I needed a miracle of healing that day and I would claim the stripes laid upon His back for my healing. As I would go about cooking and early morning breakfast for my school age children, I would sing the old song as a statement to myself: "I would not be denied, I would not be denied, 'til Jesus came and made me whole, I would not be denied." Although this became somewhat of a ritual, it was a faith-provoking one.

I have no way of knowing what the future holds, but I do know that everyday is a walk by faith in One who loves me and knows what I need. I love my Jesus and I praise Him. He did what no others could do for me! I conclude this article today with the floodgates of gratitude in my soul wide open and the tear gates of my eyes flowing. I owe to Him so very much. I *must* be about my Heavenly Father's business with renewed and retouched vigor.

Baby dedication October 18, 1970

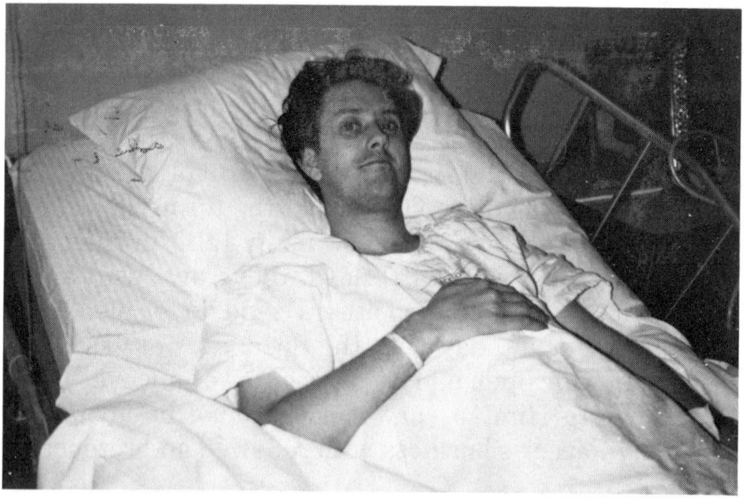

In the hospital October 30, 1970.

Four months after surgery February 20, 1971.

The family, Bill, Ann, David and Cary, 1984.

Easter, 1971

CHAPTER THIRTY

Mother Healed Of Cancer

by Mrs. A. H. Browning

This happened about the year of 1940 when we were pastors of the church in Monahans, Texas. A sister in our church, Katherine Davis, wanted me to go with her to a little place in Oklahoma to visit her folks. While in the little town of Agra, we decided that we wanted to have a revival. We were both very zealous for God and souls. We cleaned up an old unused church building and wrote two or three evangelists to see if we could get an evangelist to help us.

Our efforts to get an evangelist were in vain. As we prayed in a pasture on the day we had scheduled the start of the meeting, God gave me several messages. So I began to preach the revival. It was my beginning into the ministry. For seven nights many people attended, especially some older people who had not been to church in years.

Several times my sister in Brady, Texas called to say that my mother, Mrs. Connie Brown, was at the point of death. I really felt like continuing the revival but the calls kept insisting that if I wanted to see mother alive, I must come to Brady immediately. Sister Davis and I went to our place of prayer in an old pasture and really prayed through to victory in behalf of my mother. God gave Sister Davis a vision of my mother, whom she had never seen but when the day came that Sister Davis saw my mother in person she said it was the same woman she had seen in the vision.

I felt, however, that I had no other alternative but to close the revival and go at once to Brady. When I arrived at the Brady Hospital, my sister, who was very much opposed to my Pentecostal experience, informed me that Mother had cancer and she only had between two weeks and three months to live. She wanted us to make her as comfortable as we could and in no wise tell her of her condition. I made my sister no promises, but I told her I would be led of the Lord.

When my turn came to sit with Mother in the hospital, God led me to tell her of her condition. I will never forget when I told her. She looked up toward heaven and said, "O, do pray that I can be healed." My mother had previously received the Holy Ghost and had been baptized by Brother Browning. She was in her late sixties at that time.

The doctors had made the incision, discovered the extent of the cancer in her colon and noted the roots of the malignancy spreading into her back and legs. Sewing up the incision, they sent her home to die.

Not too long after Mother was home, a lady by the

name of Newby, who had a lot of faith in the power of the Lord, came by and prayed for Mother. Shortly after she left, Mother had a very bad sick spell and my oldest sister, who was staying with her, said the cancer passed from her body. She was troubled no more with cancer.

At the age of eighty-two she had surgery for a gall bladder trouble. One of my sisters, who is a trained nurse watched this operation. The doctors thoroughly explored Mother's stomach area and could find no trace of the former cancer problem.

I had prayed all night in our car outside the hospital prior to this operation on my mother. I talked to the doctor who performed the gall bladder surgery and he informed me he had done the surgery on my mother for the cancer problem. He said it was in the records of the hospital that my mother definitely had cancer of the colon at the time he operated. My mother lived to be almost ninety-two years of age.

Mrs. Bonnie Brown, after she was healed of cancer.

CHAPTER THIRTY-ONE

Before the Rocks Cry Out

by Carolyn Myers

Reflecting back as a child in a God-fearing family, I remember my mother quietly coming into my room in the middle of the night, kneeling by my bedside weeping and praying that God would keep His hand on me. After she would leave my room, she could be heard in my two brothers' room doing the same.

We were reared in Brother N. A. Urshan's church in Indianapolis, Indiana, and attended Calvary Christian School there. It was a sacrifice for my parents to send us to a Christian school but it was worth every cent. Many a Friday chapel services turned into revival services. I can remember some of my classmates returning home on Fridays late, but filled with the Holy Ghost.

My fourth grade found us in Seymour, Indiana where Dad accepted the pastorate of a small church.

My brother Dan felt his call into the ministry as a young teenager. He finished his high school training in

Tupelo, Mississippi and at age sixteen he asked me to go with him to preach a couple of revivals. Me! Why I was only twelve years old! We had been singing specials for quite some time and he thought this experience would be good for me. So the next few weeks were spent at the dressmaker's shop and in practicing our music.

I remember so well that warm Sunday morning pulling away from the house and waving goodbye to Mom and Dad. In their hearts they were praying: "Lord, we dedicated them for Your service. Now here they are, please take care of them."

Our first revival was with the late Elder LaFleur in Oakdale, Louisiana. Dan preached and we sang until we were hoarse, and we loved every minute of it.

The next summer my two brothers and I traveled as a trio. Sam played the standing bass, so we fit him in nicely. This time the Home Missions Department wanted us to work with the Pevers (our missionaries to the Indians in Flin Flon, Manitoba, Canada). Mom and Dad waved all three of their children goodbye and into the ministry. God's hand was on us the entire time. We had some wonderful experiences and saw some of the Indians filled with the Holy Ghost.

Dan married Ingeborg Lund, whose sister is Missionary Elsa Lund. After graduation from Apostolic Bible Institute, they evangelized a while, and during the summer months, Sam and I accompanied them. Later they pastored their first church in Flin Flon.

On one occasion Sister Wanda Nikirk, who used to travel with the late Sister Willie Johnson, held a revival for Dan. Mother, Sam and I joined them. We had services with the Indians on an island in the middle of the huge

Beaver Lake. The only transportation was by canoe. We loaded our songbooks, Bibles and instruments and rowed across. We always tried to be back to the mainland before dark. What an experience!

During this time the first sign of my trouble started. I had developed a case of chronic hives. We thought I was just allergic to something and dismissed it as that.

I went on to Bible school in St. Paul and, like most college students, I did not get the proper rest and nutrition that my body needed. In the summer of 1971 I graduated and was married in July to a wonderful man, David Myers.

We made our home in Ontario, California, and were very active in Brother Herbert Buxton's church. In December of 1972 we had a little girl, named Dava. As most new mothers I was very busy. Four months later we discovered we were expecting our second child. On January 1, 1974, my husband became the proud papa of a big brown-eyed boy. Dorian and Dava both had a lot of baby sicknesses and we were up with them more than the parents of healthy babies.

After Dorian was able to sit in his playpen, I let both the children play outdoors with me while I worked in my flower garden. It was on one of these delightful days that I thought I had sprained my wrist. For two days I had no control over it. The doctor had X-rays taken, but they did not show anything abnormal. From this time on, the pain that I had felt in my wrist spread to different joints of my body. I could never pinpoint where the pain would be on the following day. I started losing weight and my husband was forced to take over the heavier household chores. At times when my hands were weak I could not even lift the children out of the tub. I must confess, I was getting scared.

My doctor had the necessary lab work done and it showed that I had rheumatoid arthritis. I broke down and cried to the doctor and told him, "I just can't be confined to a wheelchair. I have two babies to raise."

He was sympathetic, but facts are facts and there is no cure for rheumatoid arthritis. "The only thing I can prescribe for you, Carolyn, is a pain killer."

I looked at Dr. Kartan and said, "Doctor, I believe God made my body and I'm going to trust Him to heal it."

I went home and did not take any medication for four years but as the months went by the pain intensified. During this time several major things took place in our lives. We moved twice and my husband received his call to the ministry.

Questions filled my mind as I tried to re-evaluate my life, to see if there might be any hidden things in my heart. Was God trying to purge my life through sickness? "Maybe God wants me to feel this pain so I can sympathize with others," I wondered because I always believed that with God "things don't just happen." There is a purpose and plan so that He may receive the glory.

One night in prayer I was impressed with this thought perhaps God has allowed this sickness to befall me so when He does heal me, He will get the glory. I was thrilled. I thought, "God, You have allowed me of all people to be a vessel of suffering so Your name could be glorified!" With two brothers in the ministry I had often thought what good could a woman be to God's work? It dawned on me! "Carolyn, you are being used of God so He can receive glory!" For the next two years I hugged that thought, "God, I'm grateful for this pain. I can see through Your eyes now and somehow it helps me bear it."

I had been teaching oil painting classes. One morning I met a new student with advanced arthritis. As the class progressed, the Lord spoke to me that through my sickness I would be able to witness to Pat about the Lord. Later we were able to teach her the Home Bible Study course and are anticipating her salvation.

Spring of 1980 arrived. I was very weak. My dear mother-in-law helped to hold things together. My husband had to lift me in and out of the car. I bought some little hats for church because I could not comb my hair. I did not like self-sympathy but I could not help but feel like I wasn't being fair to my husband and babies.

During this time, my resistance to sickness was very low. When my children took the flu, my body had no choice but to succumb. By the sixth week I was skin and bones, and nothing would stay on my stomach. We called my mother and asked if she could come take care of everything until I could get on my feet.

During this time I would not let myself miss church. I loved the house of God and knew folks there were praying for me and I needed the strength. I also knew that if I would miss because of a little pain, the devil would elaborate on it so I would not go at all.

One of the saints made a cushioned seat for the organ and another brought her recliner so I could sit in a little comfort. Mother and my husband took turns massaging my back and arms during the service.

Finally, I could push no further. I was confined to the bed. After much thought I went to the doctor. He took one look at the butterfly rash on my face and said, "Ah!

I believe you have what is called Systemic Lupic Erythematosus."

The cause of S.L.E. is not known at this time. It is a chronic inflammatory disease that affects the skin, joints, kidneys, nervous system, and other organs of the body. It is a great imitator of other illnesses and often takes as many as four years to diagnose. By that time some of the victims are helpless.

Approximately five out of one hundred thousand have S.L.E. and many of these do not realize it. Exposure to sunlight or ultra violet radiation often leads to the prompt appearance of a facial butterfly rash or hive-like rashes. It affects women more than men. Most victims are young women within the childbearing age. Their characteristic picture is of a patient with fever, weight loss, joint pain, fatigue, and the butterfly rash on the face. Patients develop antibodies to many of their own cells and should be treated aggressively to prevent permanent tissue injury. These treatments include rest, sun screen, physical therapy and high doses of corticosteroids.

Well, I felt hopeless (as far as man was concerned) after the doctor described all this to me. Then I began to tell him about my experience with God, how that at the age of seven years, He filled me with the Holy Ghost with the evidence of speaking in another language, and how I was baptized in the only name that remits sins, the name of Jesus.

God created me and He was acquainted with my sickness. When man does all he knows to do, God will take over.

To our astonishment, this doctor told us that he had just received the Holy Ghost and asked us if we would like to pray that God would perform a miracle in my body!

Try to visualize that office call. Dr. Tango and Mother praying for my healing and me praying for the revelation of Jesus' name to be revealed to him. I left that office weak physically but rejoicing in my spirit.

The next week I was bedfast with a raging fever. My family did not think I would live. My two brothers flew out to be with me. When they took one look at me, a prayer meeting began and it did not stop until we felt the assurance. As soon as I felt better, I asked if my neighbor, Jenny, could come over. She had been a dear friend to me.

We had had a chance to talk about the plan of salvation and she had expressed a desire to know more about it. When she walked into the room, tears filled her eyes. She could feel the overwhelming presence of God still lingering. I wanted her to be the first to know God had assured me of my healing. We wept for joy and even prayed that God would fill her with His sweet Spirit with the evidence of speaking in other tongues.

Mother felt like she could stay no longer. Being a minister's wife, she had pressing responsibilities. With a heavy heart she left for Indiana.

The next day I was admitted to Kaiser Hospital in Fontana, California. I was put on high doses of steroids and for days my condition worsened. Folks all over the country prayed for me. Then suddenly my appetite returned, the fever subsided and I began to mend.

I was hospitalized for seventeen days and I believe I had a chance to witness to seventeen nurses, two doctors, and about ten roommates. What a joy!

Dava went to Indiana to be with Mother until I could get on my feet again. One night I received a long distance call from her.

"Mommie, guess what? I just received the Holy Ghost!" The nurses were all popping their heads in the door to see what all the excitement was! That was a door opener to tell them how the Holy Ghost is still being poured out today.

After some physical therapy and learning to walk again, I was released. My husband had a three month vacation coming, so we headed to Canada. Dan, who at the time was superintendent of the Alberta-Saskatchewan district, received us warmly. It was the time of the district camp meeting. My whole family planned to be there.

Dan's family had a reason to be strong in prayer and faith in God. One night in church God had instantly and miraculously healed one of their baby twin boys of being a hydrocephalac. His head was already a third larger than the other twin's head. Today I cannot tell Mark and Tim apart.

I was too sick to attend many of the camp meeting services. I had an infection and needed to be in the hospital. Before we left, however, they carried me into the service and the congregation prayed as never before. There was tongues and interpretation saying, "Children, am I not able to raise this, my handmaiden." This aroused the church to acknowledge blessings from God such as good health.

I was once again admitted to the hospital for a trying week. This hospital was a training center. Since most of the students had never seen a lupus patient, I had plenty of company.

After being discharged I was able to return home. Granma and Granpa were waiting when we arrived. I must have looked undernourished because Granma stayed in the kitchen constantly. My appetite returned and I began to mend.

I had lost all my hair and went into a deep depression caused from a combination of the high fever, illness and medication. This was much harder for me to cope with than the lupus. At times I could not even rationalize. I needed God desperately, but I could not feel Him. I needed my pastor to encourage me, but at this time he had suddenly undergone a bypass surgery and was in much worse condition than I was. I felt trapped.

During this time, we were advised to go to a clinic out of the country which supposedly had good success with lupus patients without medication. We prayed about it. God showed my husband that if we went and any good came of it, *they* would get the glory and God will not share His glory with anyone. He wanted it all.

As we continued to pray whether to go or not, God gave Brother Buxton a dream about me. He saw a skeleton between pages of a Bible. As he turned the pages, the skeleton began to put on flesh until it was completely whole. He said, "As long as you stay in the Word of God, you will become whole!" That was the confirmation we needed. We did not go to the clinic; we trusted God.

Time is a great healer. As David and I got involved with home Bible studies and involved in others' problems, the depression gradually left, my hair came back twice as healthy, and I gained forty pounds I had lost.

In 1982 we moved to Texas to help assist in a home missions church. A specialist in Amarillo told us that he now thought that there had been a mistake. I did not have any sign of lupus!

I wanted a second opinion, so he sent me to the best rheumatologist in the nation, Dr. Don Smiley, in Dallas. I was in his office three hours. After his examination and all the tests were returned, he had the same answer as Dr. McNutt. I had some arthritis but no lupus!

My husband is now pastoring in Perryton, Texas, and I'm enjoying every minute of good health God has restored to me.

I would like to express my gratitude for the many prayers that went up on my behalf, and *before the rocks cry out,* I just want to praise the Lord for healing my body.

Sam Mena, Carolyn Mena and Dan Mena

June, 1980, before I was admitted to the hospital: lt. to rt. Dan, Mother, Carolyn, Dave and Sam.

December, 1980, hair almost gone.

The David Myers family 1985.

CHAPTER THIRTY-TWO

Thank God For My Second Voice

by John F. Pogue

A preacher with no vocal cords and no voice box.

It was June, 1978, and I had been through thirty-one cobalt treatments and four laser operations and now I was being called to the Cleveland Clinic Foundation to be told by the head of the Department for Throat and Surgery that I was going to die. But even with the hopeless news I continued to wait on the Lord.

The next four years, from 1978 to 1982, were sheer torture. I suffered headaches, earaches, insomnia, severe pain and had trouble breathing.

The more I thought it over the more I was convinced that I needed a second opinion. So I went to see another doctor. I thought maybe, just maybe, the diagnosis had been wrong. Perhaps I wasn't going to die after all. However, the second diagnosis was the same as the first and I was further told that the tumor could even spread to my brain or lungs, which meant that death was only a breath away. I didn't find out until much later that God had incased the tumor in a web so it couldn't spread. I thank God for that miracle.

Although it was a traumatic time in my life, God did not leave me alone. No, not for a moment. Reverend Nathaniel A. Urshan, the General Superintendent of the United Pentecostal Church International, had special prayer for me and told me through the power of the Holy Ghost that I was going to be around for a long time. Little did he know, at that time, how encouraging it was for me to hear him say those words. Names of friends and fellow ministers from around the world, too numerous to name one by one, prayed for me. Entire church congregations remembered me when prayer request time came. To all those wonderful friends I want to say a special thanks for being sensitive, and most of all for caring.

In May, 1982, at the Ohio District Spring Conference of the United Pentecostal Church, Brother J. Mark Jordan and Brother Joe Pearce had a deep burden from the Lord to pray for me. They, of course, were not the only ones with a burden. Many others prayed for me during that conference.

Little did I know that right after the conference my wife would have a miscarriage—another trial to add to my dilemma. Then my condition got worse. I began having a harder time breathing, so I sought medical advice again. It was at this time that I was told the opening in my throat was only the size of the point on a ballpoint pen.

The first doctor I consulted made light of my faith in God when I told him I was going to wait on the Lord, but the second doctor told me that he was going to come over to my house and see me on his way home from church. For a specialist even to mention church was a blessing; but not only that, he was going to make a house call. Miracles never cease. After he arrived he told me that I only had a few hours to live if I didn't have surgery.

It was late that Saturday night when I asked the Lord to impress someone to call me and encourage me in the direction to go. Brother Billy Cole called early the next morning because he was impressed by the Lord that he should call and talk with me. Oh, did I weep over that confirmation!

I left my home for the hospital about 5:00 a.m. and was immediately placed on oxygen to help my breathing. Although the surgery had been confirmed, in my mind I was making plans to die.

Then two sisters in the Lord from our church came to talk with me and asked me what I was going to do about my wife and children, "just in case." I became angry and told them not to talk about it. Not to even mention it. After they left my room, however, a question began to run through my mind. Would I be taking my own life if I refused to let the doctors operate, knowing that if they did there was a chance that I could live?

The decision to have the operation became final. I was going to have the cancer removed.

The doctors called it "smoker's cancer." I found that to be an amusing diagnosis since I did not smoke, but later I found out that the same kind of cancer could be caused by dust from wood, metal shavings, mold or mildew. As I began to search my mind for a time when I would have been subjected to that kind of material, my attention was drawn to the year 1977 when the church had been given a debt-free five-story bank building. It took a year to clean out the building. During that time I was exposed to dust and the other cancer-causing materials.

There I lay in a hospital room breathing from oxygen that came from a tube, yet in my heart I was still expecting God to change the picture. If only I could have seen into the future and seen the plan of God for my life. But no, I had to wait. I had to endure for a time a trial I would never forget, but one that made me stronger and better equipped to do the Lord's service as His minister.

On the day I was operated on, Brother Frank Poling from Akron came to the hospital to be by my bedside. Although I was under heavy sedation, I could feel Brother Poling's hands on my head calling on the name of Jesus.

I was in the hospital for thirty-seven days following the surgery. The healing process was very slow due to the cobalt treatments that I had undergone prior to the surgery. During my stay in the hospital, Brother J. Hugh Rose drove a long distance just to visit with me. The district superintendent of Ohio, Reverend R. A. Newstrand, also visited me during that time. Of course, my district presbyter, Reverend Paul Kearney, was a great blessing also. He continually called to find out how I was doing. Brother Frank Campbell and his wife also came to pray for me and offer their assistance. I thank God for sensitive men and women of God and a special thanks to those from the Ohio District who stood by me when I needed them most.

After I got out of the hospital I had to have eleven more operations. But during that time, even sometimes with tubes in my nose, I taught Sunday school and midweek Bible classes on an overhead transparency. Because

I could not talk it took hours to prepare my lesson and get it across to the congregation. Even so, I was home and doing God's will for my life and I loved it. You should have seen the faces of the audience when I took the pointer and instead of reading, had my brother, Reverend Randy Pogue, read for me.

Then my presbyter, Reverend Paul Kearney, handed me an article about a new voice device that could be inserted into the windpipe. It was a plastic tube that actually helped produce words. When I inquired about this new device, I was told that I could learn to speak by learning how to gulp air and then develop the gulping of air into words.

It had been done before and I got the chance to hear someone do it, but it seemed very difficult. I couldn't even imagine trying to give a half-hour sermon with this new technique. All I could think of was lying on the floor completely out of breath after a sermon. After all, I was a Pentecostal preacher, if you know what I mean. So, at first this new-fangled idea was not feasible.

However, after much consideration and prayer, even though I knew of some instances where people were unsuccessful with this new device, I consulted my doctor to see if he would do whatever necessary for me to have it. To my amazement he was dead set against it. He told me it would never work and he did not want to do it. That did not deter me, however; I went ahead and made arrangements to go to Indianapolis, Indiana, to have the surgery necessary to use this new plastic device.

When my doctor found out that I was determined to have the plastic tube inserted with or without his consent, he said, "O.K. Reverend Pogue. I'll do it." Well, after six attempts and much discouragement and depression, it finally worked.

Presently I am being asked to visit hospitals and encourage other patients, like myself, so that they may have a new hope of a new beginning, just as I have. I am making an hour cassette tape recording for Fairview Hospital so that others having this same surgery, wondering if they'll ever be able to talk again, will hear my new voice and be lifted up.

It is very possible that soon I will make a video tape at the Cleveland Clinic Foundation to help patients there. To God be the praise and the glory. I serve on the Ohio Commission on Aging and the Mayor's Commission on Aging in Cleveland, Ohio, which I might add is a great honor. But what a testimony this ordeal has been to them of God's miraculous power and the determination He has given me to not only live for Him but continue to do His wonderful work!

Now, for the icing on the cake so to speak. I have a new voice. I call it my second voice and I can preach and teach with this new voice. But that isn't all. I am able to do something under the anointing of the Lord that no one else with an artificial voice has ever done: I can sing. WOW! what the Lord can do! Speaking in tongues as the Spirit gives utterance? You better believe it. God hasn't changed and neither has His Spirit, and as long as the Spirit of God continues to work in my life, speaking in tongues goes without saying, even with my second voice.

My testimony here is to encourage you to trust in the Lord, to have faith in God. There isn't anything He cannot do. My testimony, if I could sum it up, would be thus: "Having obtained help from God, I can continue until this day." No matter what the circumstances, we should never ask God, "Why me?" Instead, we should just praise the Lord and say, "Father, be glorified."

May I ask you a question? How would you like to be in my shoes and to have gone through what I went through for the last few years? As a preacher I could have been justified to quit. But I thank God for the burdens that I still have for the city of Cleveland.

God has made me a "walking, talking miracle." Oh, thanks to the Lord for my second voice!

To all my family and friends, I say thank you; to the congregation God has placed me over, I say I love and appreciate you; but to the Lord Jesus Christ, I say "Forever I am Yours to do Your will whatever that may be. Thank You, Lord, for my second voice."

Rev. John F. Pogue

CHAPTER THIRTY-THREE

Healed of Cancer of the Eye

by Harvey Lee Price

About four years ago I went for new glasses. When the doctor examined my eyes, he told my wife to see that I got to a eye specialist.

I went that very day to Dr. Barnes, who examined my eyes closely. Then he said, "You have cancer in your right eye. I want you to go to Harmon Hospital to see another specialist. His name was Dr. Ruiz."

Before I went to see Doctor Ruiz, I went to church. Brother O. R. Fauss and the church prayed for me. When I went the next day to the Harman Hospital, Doctor Ruiz examined my eyes carefully. He also told me I had cancer. "The name of the cancer is melanoma. That is the worst kind of cancer and it is in a place where I cannot treat it, so I will have to take the eye out."

But I refused. "No, I can't let you take my eye out. We will pray that my Lord will heal my eye," I replied.

I know Doctor Ruiz thought I was crazy. He nevertheless gave me an appointment to be back in three months. "If the cancer has gotten larger I will have to take the eye out," he affirmed.

On the third month I went back for my appointment. As Doctor Ruiz checked me this time, he kept looking into my eye. Then he said, "It is smaller."

"I told you it would be smaller or gone," I replied.

"I want to see you again in two months," the doctor insisted.

After two months I went back. Doctor Ruiz checked my eye over and over again. Then the doctor said, "Well, it's gone."

But the good doctor wasn't satisfied. He wanted to run a dye test and take more pictures. But the dye test did not reveal any cancer.

"Even though it is not there, I want you back in six months," Doctor Ruiz insisted.

When six months passed, I went back. Doctor Ruiz checked very carefully, but there was no trace of the cancer.

Doctor Ruiz told me, "I should have listened to you at first and you wouldn't have had to go through all these check-ups."

"When my Lord does anything it is done right," I answered Doctor Ruiz.

This story is true for it happened to me.

CHAPTER THIRTY-FOUR

My God Heals

by Berthal Crossno

It was the season of the year that I like most, the month of May. After the winter months I like to get outside. I pastored a church not far from my home and did quite a bit of visiting among the members.

It had been a week since the doctor had removed a mole from the calf of my right leg when the telephone rang. One of the nurses from the hospital said, "Dr. Butterworth wants to speak to you."

"Berthal, that thing was malignant, and I want you to come in this afternoon for further surgery tomorrow."

"I don't know what I want to do," I hesitated.

"You make up your mind and if you decide to, call in and we'll reserve you a bed."

My first reaction was to start crying. My world had suddenly fallen apart! This could happen to anyone else but not to me! After I told my husband what the doctor said, we knelt together and prayed. While in prayer my anxiety left. Everything was calm in my spirit. Whichever way the Lord wanted the pendulum to swing was all right with me.

The doctor told me the type of cancer was melanoma. My sister-in-law had died with this type of cancer and I knew it would not be long for me unless God intervened. The doctor said the cancer was not in the blood but was carried by the blood and could break out in any part of the body.

I told my husband that I owed it to him and our thirteen-year-old adopted son, Dale, to do all I could. I entered the Benton County General Hospital that evening. Word spread and people went to prayer. The doctor said he could do drastic surgery and take out the nodes or local surgery and take out a portion surrounding the place from which he had taken the mole. I chose the latter. The doctor removed a large piece of flesh and grafted skin from my thigh on it. The grafted skin healed except a place about the size of a silver dollar.

"Cobalt will not help this type of cancer since it is carried by the blood," the doctor said. He prescribed hydrea, a medication to be taken orally.

Later a lump came on my upper chest wall. The Doctor suggested removing the growth which he did. When the laboratory results came in, he told us that it was the same cancer. The news was not pleasant, but I felt the peace of God in my heart.

I said, "Doctor Butterworth, I have lived for this hour. I have had the Holy Ghost for forty-three years and I have been preaching the gospel for forty years."

"You are ready then" he smiled.

"Yes, I want you to meet me," I answered firmly.

"I hope to" was his reply.

I continued taking the hydrea for sometime, but it pulled my white corpuscles. I was very weak it was difficult for me to keep going. When time came for our camp meeting, I wanted to go.

"Let me leave off the medication so I can go to camp," I requested of the doctor.

"We'll try it," he agreed.

My husband, Dale Okley, took the week off from work to attend camp. The presence of the Lord was wonderful. One night Brother Greer asked the ministers to form two lines far enough apart for those who wanted prayer to walk through. The ministers laid their hands on us as we walked through the prayer line. Immediately I knew something had happened.

When we came home from camps I didn't take the hydrea. Soon I was back in the pulpit preaching. Many tests have been made since, but if any trace of the cancer symptoms have shown up, they have not told me. The doctor did say, "The Lord has done something for you."

At St. Thomas Hospital in Nashville they ran tests but there was still no cancer. I am now seventy-three years old. I resigned the pastorate of the church after twenty-one years as their pastor, effective in 1978.

After fifty-four years in the ministry and seeing God work miracle after miracle, my only regret is that I do not have another life to give to the work of the Lord.

CHAPTER THIRTY-FIVE

Against All Odds

by Tracy Boutlier

Dr. Pritchard pushed back his chair, looked up from the test results he was evaluating, adjusted his glasses and with a pixy grin on his face, "Reverend, I don't know just what we are going to do with you."

I fidgeted a little, attempted to clear my throat and half stammered, "And what is that supposed to mean."

"It means, my friend," he replied punctuating each phrase with verbal exclamation marks, "that your case has defied every odd of this hospital. You are not supposed to be alive today. When you came your case was totally hopeless, but here you are alive, and in spite of the odds it looks as though you will be around for some time to come."

The setting of this life and death drama is The M. D. Anderson Cancer and Tumor Research Institution of Houston, Texas, one of the largest and most prestigious institutions in the world.

After a routine physical examination by Dr. Walter Asseff of Shreveport, Louisiana, I was sent to Dr. James Bergeron, also of the same city, a skin specialist who took biopsies and sent them to several pathologists for analysis. I was then given the awful verdict that in about six weeks I would be a dead man.

Diagnosis: Malignant melanoma, which had already metastasized. Two hairless slate black melanoma about six inches to the left of my backbone belt high and a large double tumor which resembled a mushroom about an inch from the backbone on the same side of the melanoma. An R. N. fled the room after seeing the monster and went into an adjoining office stating that she had just witnessed the most awful sight she had ever seen.
Prognosis: Melanoma is one of the fastest growing and most deadly of all cancers. Prognosis is extremely poor. In fact, there is no sure way to tell which way it will go. It is a cunning, capricious enemy. Dr. Fair measured on my back for my wife, Rachel, showing how much would have to be excised. Her response was that they could not do that, to which he completely agreed. I was told much later that the doctors had given serious consideration to not attempting to do anything at all. The case was beyond hope, the treatment would be too severe, too horrible and totally worthless. But being the good doctors they are, they had to try. So they referred me to M. D. Anderson. These great learned men were of the same mind as the ones in Shreveport; the case was hopeless. Nevertheless they tried.

For over a week I was given all the sophisticated tests

they deemed necessary. After the tests I found myself in a small, white room all alone; a cold, white, impersonal place it was. A shiver slowly passed through my frame as I wondered what stories of fear and pain and hopelessness, and, too, of surprise and relief this room could tell if it could only talk. In a few minutes now I would know the worst and best I could expect.

Alone? Not really. Another presence was in the room with me that day. I had talked to God and He had listened. I have been a preacher of the gospel since my teen years, and one thing I have learned well is that you do not make deals with God. You go His way or you don't go with Him at all.

My prayer went something like this, "Dear, great almighty God I do not know how much time I have left here, but You do. Father, I am today renewing the commitment I made with You so many years ago, when I was just a lad, and You chose me to work for You. Whether little or much I will use it all in Your service. I am not trying to strike a bargain; my time is in your hands."

It was not long before a half dozen or so of the most knowledgeable doctors in the world entered the room bearing results of the most advanced examinations possible. Apparently the leader of the group was Dr. Charles McBride, reputed to be one of the foremost authorities on melanoma in the world. In counsel with the others, he would prescribe whatever treatment they thought might do some good, although they were sure nothing would really work. Dr. Michael Andrew Burgess, the head of chemotherapy, was present together with the chiefs of other departments of this institution. The melanoma had already begun to metastasize (scatter). At that very moment they knew it was doing its deadly work throughout my body.

But wait! They had not brought into focus the hand of God who was doing a mighty work in that cancer-ridden body.

To the utter astonishment of everyone of them, they could find no trace of the disease in any organ. Still, they insisted. It had to be lurking somewhere in the body and sooner or later it would show its ugly self.

M. D. Anderson is a research institution, and that day I became a research patient. Henceforth, I would be known as experiment case number 115-777.

There was a new course of treatment they wanted to try, so I, with about five others, was assigned to this experiment. First I received ten days of deep immunotherapy. This consisted of split injections of C Parvum; following this five days of D.T.I.C. this is chemotherapy given intravenously.

There are some cruel side effects of chemotherapy. Believe me when I say there is no way to convey the sheer nauseating horror of the awful treatment. It may work; many times it backfires and causes the tumor to grow; then again there is always the chance that the treatment will kill the patient. It is the worst treatment known to man. I have had fifty rounds.

My case was similar to Apostle Peter's when he was arrested and put in prison. James had been killed with the sword and now Peter was in prison awaiting death on the morning. But prayer was made without ceasing of the church unto God for him. The Almighty has something to say in these matters; and in both cases, He said it loud and clear.

I do not know who prayed the prayer of faith for me. There is no way to tell. Who touched is not important, but the fact that He was touched is all important. So to God be the praise and the glory! It is a fact that every dear one who prayed for me received a positive answer. And the number who prayed were legion. I know my darling wife, Rachel, interceded for me without ceasing.

One of the most heartwarming incidents of that dark day was brought about by my preacher son, Robin, who was overheard by his mother one day as he was weeping and calling on God in the garage, for my healing. He said, "Oh, God, if You are going to take my daddy home, please let his mantle fall on me." It is enough to say that prayer was made by the church unto God, as was made by the twenty-four hour prayer chain at Irvington Pentecostal Church in Houston, Texas.

Allow me at this point to express my undying gratitude to Reverend C. L. Dees and his lovely wife Marvelle, together with Brother Johnny and Zula Mott for their open hearts and homes for the better part of a year.

My case was contrary to all that was known about melanoma. Something was working of such monumental proportions as to excite such statements as this. One day after the operation, and it looked as though I might get well, Dr. Morris asked me to whom was I going to give credit for what was happening, Dr. McBride or faith. I didn't even have to think about it; I told him that the first credit went to God and if there was any left I would give it to Dr. McBride. To this he replied, and I quote, "Reverend, we don't deserve any credit. The truth is, it is nothing we have done. For your case there was no cure."

I asked Dr. Powell, who looked after me for a while, what the odds were on me getting well when I first came to M.D. Anderson. He squinted his eyes for a long moment as if in deep thought. "In all the world you may find a case such as yours, but I would say that this hospital considered your case 100% fatal. Doctors outside of institutions such as this never see things like this. My personal thought is that what has happened here is 99% faith."

Dr. Richmond, who was one of the department chiefs present when the first decisions were made, said as he looked at a picture of my back, "This photograph has become a very famous picture in this hospital."

One day as he was examining my back, Dr. Bergeron said, "Reverend, I used your case in a seminar the other day at L.S.U.S. (Louisiana State University, Shreveport). I was giving a lecture on melanoma, and at the end of my lecture I told them I had something special to show. I slipped a 'before' slide of your back into the projector and flashed it up on the screen. I let them absorb this for a while as we commented on what a deadly thing we were looking at. I then flashed an 'after' picture on the screen. They sat transfixed as I did, 'And that, class, is what faith will do.' " Before this the good doctor did not much believe in miracles, but every time I walk into his office now he calls me the miracle man and advises his clients to pray. Today he has evidence that Jesus Christ is the healer.

November 11, 1980, is a day long to be remembered. It happened this way. After Dr. Powell had evaluated the tests, he went to read the X-rays and returned with Dr. Burgess. Upon entering, Dr. Burgess placed his arm around my shoulder and said, "Well, Reverend, this is it."

I knew what he meant but decided to play a little game with him, so I feigned a degree of fear. I suppressed a shout and asked, "What do you mean? You know that could mean a number of things."

"I mean," he said smiling broadly (this was unusual for him for he is a very serious, sober man), "that you are a well man. We dismiss you today. All immuno stops as of now. We never thought the day would come, but there it is. Go home, live your life, do what you wish, you are a well man."

Dr. Powell added, "You should never be bothered with this again."

We exchanged goodbyes and I stepped out into the crowded hall to join my friend, Reverend Reginald Dees, who had come with me for these tests.

I paused for a moment and told Reginald that there was something I had to do before I left. We were in a jammed waiting room. Quite loudly I said, "Everyone, your attention, please. I have to tell you. Four years ago I came to this place to die. I had melanoma in the worst way (they all knew what that meant); today, just a few minutes ago, Dr. Burgess pronounced me well and dismissed me. I must tell you there is hope; you must have faith. My case was considered hopeless but today I am a well man. Believe me there is hope!"

There was one last stop I wanted to make. I had to tell Marty the good news and say goodbye. Marty was the head of the skin testing department and the one person I had more dealings with than any other. Marty was busy as usual, but she took time out to chat a bit and recall some of the past four years. I asked her what chance she thought I had four years ago. Her answer was an unqualified "None." Our farewells were words of victory and victories do not happen often here. Some new patients were waiting to take their first skin tests, so we talked loud enough for them to hear so that hopefully a little light would shine down that dark way they had yet to travel.

We made our way down the crowded halls past filled waiting rooms, turned in my case file and stepped out into the brisk November evening air. I was anxious to get home now. There were things to do, people to help. Almighty God had extended my life and I had every intention of finding out His purpose for me and a firm resolve to do it. I well remember the last words of Dr. Burgess when I referred to my disease in the past tense, "That's the way to say it, 'I had melanoma but I don't have it anymore.' "

I first went to Houston, Texas, to M. D. Anderson on the fifteenth of January 1976. Today is November the seventh, 1984.

Twice a week Rachel and I go to Marthaville, Louisiana, a tiny village in northwest Louisiana to minister the gospel of the salvation of the Lord Jesus Christ to a small flock of God's children in a beautiful little church called Calvary Temple.

Bro. & Sis. Tracy Boutlier

CHAPTER THIRTY-SIX

Healed Of Cancer

by Lester Thompson

My mother, Doris Mae Thompson, was born in Lucas, Iowa, in the year 1900. Her earliest contact with Pentecost was at the age of six years when she attended revival services being conducted by Brother and Sister Howard A. Goss in her home town.

At that early age she loved to attend church and did so while growing up. It was not until 1928, however, that she received the wonderful experience of baptism in the name of Jesus Christ and the infilling of the Holy Ghost. From this experience came a great faith for divine healing. She was healed of many afflictions during her lifetime.

On one occasion, as a teenager, I remember Mother lying in bed and turning blue. I rushed to our pastor across the street to ask for prayer. Brother D. D. Dainty came immediately. Prayer was offered and in a matter of minutes Mother was up, dancing in the Spirit and her color was back to normal.

The real test of faith came in 1948 when Mother found that she had incurable cancer. She was taking treatments at the time, but was growing steadily worse and was almost bedridden. Living one-half block from the church, she asked to be taken to the service for prayer. She was carried to the church, Bethel Tabernacle in Racine, Wisconsin.

Pastor L. R. Mitchell and the saints prayed and believed God for a miracle. The pastor asked God for a sign to prove that she, indeed, was healed and the sign was for her to arise and dance in the Spirit. She did so, beautifully and unmistakenly proving that the Lord had removed the cancer from her body.

My mother walked from the church that night to her home. She returned no more to the doctor for exams or treatments. She lived for twenty-eight more years without ever having a reoccurrence of the dread disease. The saints and ministers in the Racine area often used this miracle to encourage others to believe God no matter how serious their illness may be.

CHAPTER THIRTY-SEVEN

The Touch of the Velvet Hand

by Libby Fink

Rose Thomas was grateful for the job that God had supplied during World War II. She quickly dressed for work and kissed her mother goodbye. Periodically the employees at the Universal Match Company in Ferguson, Missouri, had to pass a security and health check. This was among the least of Rose's worries. She was often very tired, but she had credited the fatigue to the lack of food. They were very poor and Rose often gave her share of the food to her ailing mother.

Rose was attempting to push thoughts of hunger out of her mind when she received news that her X-rays would have to be retaken. Heartsick she lifted her chin and proceeded to be X-rayed. The extra days off with pay did not seem to ease the fear of the results.

Too soon she was given the verdict. The dreaded tuberculosis was in both of her lungs. Her employment was terminated and she was advised to move because of the fumes and the pollution. Soon the bags were packed and the two women were bound for Pacific, Missouri, where they owned property.

Faithfully every afternoon Rose would walk to a small creek which drained across their property and cast some bread crumbs into the water and pray. She grew weaker, but she insisted that one of her relatives walk her to the creek to "cast her cares on the waters." Her relatives tried to cooperate merely to humor her because of her failing health.

This ritual continued until a second summer shone upon the St. Louis area. The little Apostolic church at Forest and Bruno, where Rose had become a member shortly before her tragic discovery, had been praying for her each service. Then God burdened one of the men. He suggested that the church fast a week for Sister Rose Thomas and another sister who had cancer.

Rose continued steadfastly in her faith unaware of the additional prayer and fasting that was petitioning the Lord on her behalf. She continued to gain strength. At the beginning of the fast she walked four long blocks into town to be X-rayed by her physician. The tuberculosis had not diminished, but the physician was encouraged that she was capable of walking that distance without wheezing and that she no longer needed assistance.

Late that afternoon Rose walked to the bridge and cast her usual bread offering plus an additional little cake that she had made. She prayed for her friends and family as well as her church back in the city on Forest and Bruno. Then she added, "Now, Jesus, I've taken my share of the flour for tomorrow and made this small cake as the widow made for Elijah. I offer it in faith believing that You will supply our need for food and You will heal me as You have said in Your Word. By Your stripes, I am healed! I accept my healing now, Amen." The crumbs were cast into the water. She returned home and went to bed.

She was awakened late the next morning when her neighbor knocked on the door. She wanted to know if the women needed anything from town. The mother merely requested that she bring back their mail. The aged woman had too much pride to admit that they did not even have three cents to purchase a stamp to let the family know that they had no food or fuel.

Later that afternoon voices could be heard in the yard. Rose's aged mother peeked out the curtain. Her neighbors were headed toward the house with arms loaded with groceries. The ladies in town had been impressed to send the Thomases some groceries. This was enough food to last weeks! The Lord had provided once again!

After supper, Rose was drawn outside by the coolness of the evening. She walked along the creek bank praising God for the food that He had provided. Suddenly there was a presence that surrounded her. She was no longer alone. "Rose, Rose," a Voice interrupted her thoughts. "Rose, you had faith that I would send you and your mother food. Rose, do you really want to be healed?"

Rose replied, "Yes. Yes, Lord, You know I do!" Then the Voice asked, "Rose, why do you cast bread in the creek each day?" Rose responded, "Ecclesiastes 11:1, 'Cast thy bread upon the waters: for thou shalt find it after many days.' I need to cast my needs as well as my problems on the Lord. Left in His hands, He'll take care of my needs. My answer will come to me at the needed moment." Then Rose added, "I'm casting my cares and my needs on the water. Lord, I want to serve You and I can't do very much for You in my present condition."

"Rose, if you want your healing, all that you have to do is to raise your arms."

This was an impossible task to ask of Rose. She was incapable of raising her arms above her head as a result of her condition. She responded, "Lord, I can't raise my arms. I. . . ." The Lord asked the impossible so that she would have to reach out by obedience and faith to accomplish this request. Her faith would heal her, as the man with the withered hand (see Mark 3:1-5) was healed when he surpassed the impossible to stretch forth his hand in obedience to Jesus' command.

The Lord once again responded, "Rose, I told you what to do." He didn't want to hear excuses that she couldn't physically do it. He came to heal her.

Rose understood. "I'll do it!" She raised her arms to heaven to praise her Creator for her healing. There was no pain! This was the first time that she was capable of raising her arms without excruciating pain and without choking spasms.

Something beautiful happened that day. Instead of the searing pain in her chest, Rose felt as if God was wearing a soft velvet glove and wiping each lung from top to bottom. All pain ceased instantaneously. She could breathe! She was healed! The young woman who had laboriously walked to the creek began running, shouting, and praising God for the touch of the Master's hand. She was revived with new life and new hope.

That same night God moved on the Apostolic church at Forest and Bruno. One of the members testified that

God had just impressed upon them that Sister Rose Thomas had received her healing that afternoon. Praise the Lord for a congregation who is sensitive enough to let God work through them!

The next morning Rose quickly dressed. As she was sipping her hot milk, her mother came into the kitchen. Rose told her, "Mother, I'm going to see Dr. Macknay. I want new X-rays."

"Rose, we don't have the money to pay for them," her mother explained.

"Mom, God will provide," Rose responded with faith.

Shortly, Rose left for the physician's office. She was a new woman. She no longer had to struggle to walk. She briskly passed the creek and off she flew. As soon as she arrived, she asked the physician to X-ray her once again. By faith she pledged to pay him after she received her mail.

At first the physician was reluctant. He had just taken the annual X-rays required of tuberculosis victims. Rose proceeded to explain how the velvet glove of God had wiped her lungs clean. Finally, the physician agreed, but merely to humor her.

As the X-rays were being developed, Rose trotted to the Post Office. Several of the saints from the church at Forest and Bruno in Maplewood had written her. As she opened her mail, tears began to trickle down her cheeks. Each letter contained a few dollars. Praise God, He had provided once again. It was more than sufficient.

When she arrived at the physician's office again, he said that he wanted to retake the X-rays that he had just taken. She replied that she only had enough money to pay for the first X-rays with enough money for food for two days. She simply did not have enough money for an additional X-ray.

Her physician firmly replied, "I'm not going to charge you for this retake. If I find what I think I just found. . . ." His voice faded into a murmur that was not understandable. Rose knew why the physician wanted an additional X-ray. It was all that she could do to restrain herself from dancing before the Lord in worship for her healing. The X-rays were taken and she waited for the results.

The door slowly opened. A frown was plastered on the physician's face as he slowly walked through the door. Scratching his head while he viewed the results, the physician asked, "Rose, did you ever have chicken pox, small pox or measles?"

"Yes, sir. I had the measles," she cheerfully responded.

The physician continued, "Rose, that means you have been freed from the tuberculosis that has bound you. You have been healed. Would you like to tell me again how God has healed you?"

That was the opportunity that Rose had been waiting for all day. She related her testimony to him again.

After several X-rays, blood tests, and much paper work, Rose was officially declared healed of tuberculosis. There remained a special glow on Rose's face as she testified of her healing every opportunity that she received through the years. She loved her God. She served Him with every ounce of energy that she had.

My life has been enriched by the strength that Rose has shown. It was difficult to let her go when God called her home some thirty years after He healed her of tuberculosis. I am grateful that God let our paths cross, for

I have learned so much from my Great Aunt Rose Thomas' walk as she went through life hand in hand with God who wore the velvet glove.

Lt. to Rt. Rose Thomas with sisters Pearl and Mary, and Mother Annie.

CHAPTER THIRTY-EIGHT

Elena

By Mollie Thompson

She was a repulsive sight, open sores and scaly skin covered her body so that even the other lepers in "Agua de Dios" studiously avoided her. A lonely, embittered and unwanted soul. . .but a soul nevertheless. She wandered around the streets of Colombia's Leper Colony alone.

Life had no interest for Elena. The free cinema shows lost their appeal, the cheap cigars she bought at the Comisariato lost their taste, and the beer that was distributed so liberally in the tavern tasted more like ditch water every day.

"What is there to live for?" she often asked herself, "if this existence can be called living?"

Many times she had considered taking her life, but each time she had tried to do so she found herself shaken by doubts and fears about what lay beyond the door of death. "Purgatory" the priest told her, was the place where the sins taken with a person from this life were burned away, and from there the soul went to heaven. But it took money and moneyed friends to pay the way out of purgatory, and she possessed neither.

She wandered disconsolately down the main street of the town trying not to notice how almost everyone avoided contact with her. When she saw how they passed her, she either glared at them in self defense or screamed obscenities after them. She burned with the knowledge that for her there was no hope.

On one of her trips down to the tavern she was surprised to hear a voice speaking to her. She looked up bewildered into the smiling eyes and kindly face of a stranger. Without a trace of revulsion in his expression, he handed her a paper saying gently, "Read this. It will help you."

Wonderingly, she took the paper and asked, "Can *anything* or *anyone* help me?"

"Not *anyone*, but *someone*," was the reply.

"Who? What's his name? Tell me, sir." In her anxiety she stretched out her hand and grasped his coat sleeve, forgetting that he might resent her touch, but he didn't. She dropped her hand hurriedly to her side, He answered her again in the same gentle voice. "His name is Jesus." With that the man was gone.

She took the paper home deciding that if it did her no good it could do her no harm. As she read the paper, her heart was warmed within her. It was a simple story of a Savior who had died and risen from the dead. She found within herself a longing to know about Him.

"The stranger told me that His name is Jesus," she said to herself. "I had better go and find out all I can about Him."

The little paper had an address at the bottom telling her where to go should she desire to know more. She did want to know more.

At the risk of being shunned, she went to the address given and found herself at the door of a small house where quite a number of people most of them lepers, were gathered. Seating herself on the back row, she listened as the gospel message in all its beauty was unfolded.

The preacher never had a more attentive listener than Elena, and even as the tears rolled unheeded down her cheeks she knew that unclean as she was physically, she was far more unclean spiritually.

"I must be baptized," was the uppermost thought in her mind. Then with stunning reality came the thought, "Who will baptize me?" After the service she made her way, howbeit cautiously, still afraid of being shunned, to the preacher and asked him to baptize her.

In Colombia the baptizer enters the water with the candidate. The preacher was very reluctant to do so. He had a legitimate excuse and hurriedly he produced it. "I am not licensed to baptize," he said. "I only have a local license."

"However, I will call the missionary. He'll come and baptize you."

Brother Thompson received the call from the worker that one of the lepers wanted to be baptized in Jesus' name. He packed his overnight case and left Bogota on the early morning bus.

He told me later that he was shocked at her appearance, but he did not allow his feelings to come through.

"Do you really understand what you are doing?" he

asked.

"Yes," she answered with tear-filled eyes. "I must be cleansed from my sins." A curious crowd had gathered to watch in fascinated horror as Bill climbed into the tank and then turned and held out his hand to help Elena in. The people were unable to understand why the "Gringo" would take such a risk.

The powerful words were pronounced, "Elena, sobre la confesion de tu fe te bautizo en el nombre de Jesuscristo para perdon de los pecados," and with that he plunged her beneath the water.

Scales of skin and other refuse from her broken body floated on the top of the water and clung to Bill's clothes, but he simply climbed out and made his way to the meeting place where he changed, leaving the clothes he used for baptism behind. The law forbade them to be taken back to the capital city.

Elena was never able to fully express how she felt as she came up out of the waters of baptism. She only knew that she spoke in a language she did not understand and that nothing mattered anymore but Jesus. She had never felt so happy, and the fact that people continued to avoid her as she went home did not rouse her to a frenzy as it formerly did.

She went to bed that night and slept the sleep of a little child. When she awoke and started to take the sheet from her bed, she noticed that the sheet, which was usually soaked with pus, blood and scales of skin, was clean. She could hardly believe her eyes. She ran to her little lean-to kitchen where a mirror hung on the wall. As she looked, she screamed, and screamed. Her face was clean, the sores had vanished! The scales had dropped off! Then the realization came over her that she had been cleansed, not only inside but also outside.

"I'm clean, I'm clean," she screamed. The neighbors came running. "Look, look," she extended her hands, showed them her head, laughing and weeping with joy she ran from house to house, all the time shouting, "Oh God, I'm clean, I'm clean." Her flesh, like that of Naaman's had become as that of a little child.

Three weeks later, pronounced clean by the authorities, she walked the streets of Bogota announcing to all who would listen that "Jesus Christ is the same, yesterday, today and forever."

One thing still remains a mystery to us. Who was the *stranger* who gave her the tract?

Rev. and Mrs. Thompson

CHAPTER THIRTY-NINE

No Toys On Credit

by Paul Ray Cagle, Jr.

Black Thursday, October 25, 1929, marked the beginning of one of the darkest periods financially for the United States. It was known as the day the market crashed, the beginning of the Great Depression.

Those living at that time will never forget the memories of their hardships endured during this era. Banks failed and men went from riches to rags overnight. Fortunes and life-savings were completely wiped-out. The rich stood in the bread-line with the poor. In Chicago, Illinois, fifty men scrambled in the garbage behind one restaurant just for something to eat. It was estimated that one hundred thousand children roamed the streets and highways. And the suicide rate was at an unbelievable high.

Down in the rural areas of Tennessee, people were feeling the effects of the Depression as well, although it was not as severe as in the urban areas across America.

The Cagle house was bustling with the excitement and spirit of the holiday season as Christmas approached that year. The "wishbook" *Sears, Roebuck Catalog* had just arrived. What a treat it was to study every page of that wonderful book, especially the section marked "toys."

"Honey," Sister Nettie Cagle approached her preacher husband, "I know our income is meager, and our budget is very limited, but it's been so long since our children have received a store-bought toy. Can't we be extravagant just this once and order a toy for each of them?"

Nettie had noticed how little Nadine had wrapped an old milk bottle in a blanket and caressed it to her breast like a baby doll.

With a heart full of love for his little family, Odell realized the many hardships and sacrifices his family had made. "Sure, Nettie. I don't see what harm there is in splurging this time; besides, this is Christmas."

With permission for the order to be made, the young mother gathered the children to her. "Now children, you may select one toy from the 'wish-book'."

"I want this doll baby," cried Nadine.

"This B.B. gun is just for me!" exclaimed Aaron.

"I want an airplane, just like Lucky Lindy flies," announced Sam.

"And I pick this pair of skates," the baby Paul decided.

With all their selections made, Sister Cagle carefully made out the order, stuck it in the envelope, hunted everywhere until a stamp was found, and mailed it. She had failed to read all the small print at the bottom of the order sheet, which read, *"No toys on credit."*

Preparations were made for the holiday season, but no packages arrived. As the days slipped into weeks, still no packages. Everyday the children made their pilgrimage to the Post Office and asked the clerk behind the counter, "Anything for the Cagles?" And everyday they received the same answer from the old postmaster who would smile sympathetically.

Finally, Sister Cagle began to wonder about the order. When she took out her copy, she realized her terrible mistake; at the bottom of the order sheet in small print, she read *"No toys on credit."*

"How careless of me," she cried, as she searched for a way she could break the sad news to her four anxious children. "Children, will you all come in here for a minute," the heart-broken mother began. "I have some bad news. There will be no toys for Christmas this year." As she continued, she briefly explained the oversight on her part.

All the Christmas joy vanished. The shock was more than the children could bear. Their cries went up all over the house. "No toys! No toys."

But where was little Paul?

The five-year-old baby of the Odell Cagle family had quietly slipped out of the room, moved down the hall, into his bedroom, and shut the door. He had instantly remembered something that his parents had taught him. Quietly and reverently, without being noticed, little Paul knelt beside his bed and prayed a simple prayer. "Jesus, my momma and daddy told me that what we ask in Your name, You will do it. Please make that man send us our toys. In Jesus' name. Amen." With that he left his room and announced to the others, "You all can quit your crying now. Jesus is sending us our toys."

A child's simple prayer. A parent's faithful teaching about faith. It truly must have touched the very heart of God. Not many days later, a package arrived for the Cagle children. And it did include all the toys Sister Cagle had ordered.

A note from the president of the company read, "It is against our company's policy to send toys on credit during these hard times, but for some unknown reason I feel to make this one exception. May yours be a very Merry Christmas."

It was a lesson in faith that the Cagle children would never forget, and a Christmas that would be special for years to come.

God not only answered the important needs for "daily bread" during those hard times. But in this case He added some extra blessings, all because a little child believed.

Paul Cagle 1936 Newbern, Tennessee.

The Cagle children 1933, lt. to rt. Nadine, Sam, Aaron and Little Paul.

CHAPTER FORTY

A New Heart

by Bruce T. Allen

My wife, Sharon, had been praying for some time for God to increase her faith. Little did she realize the actions God would use to fulfill her prayer.

On August 31, 1984, while eating the noon meal, I suffered severe problems with breathing, also my left arm became numb. I laid on the sofa but became worse. Our family doctor recommended that I come to his office.

He immediately admitted me to the ICU of the hospital. After getting me calmed down, he did an EKG test and it showed damage to my heart. The blood test showed enzymes being released due to heart damage. I spent one week in ICU and another week in the regular care ward. During this time all EKG testing showed heart damage. An Echocardiagram also showed damage.

The third day of my hospital stay was Sunday morning. The nurse came to take my blood sample to check for blood enzymes. I told her that great men had prayed for me in Jesus' name and she wouldn't find any enzymes. After that morning, no more enzymes from heart damage could be found. I believe that was the beginning of my healing.

After being released from the hospital, my diagnosis was two months at home doing nothing! That was a tough order for one having been so active in the ministry. I experienced depression like I'd never known before—questioning everything. After about a week of this, I'd had enough. I gave it all to the Lord and told the devil that the "joy of the Lord is my strength." After that night, I accepted the fact that I'd had a heart attack but that God would see me through—and He did!

After seven weeks, I was sent to Mayo Clinic in Rochester, Minnesota, for three days of further heart testing. Up until this time, all the tests were showing heart damage. More blood tests, EKG's and a heart catherization were done at Mayo Clinic.

Thursday morning when I arrived at Mayo Clinic, they did an EKG. That afternoon, I met with the doctor for consultation. He told me that the EKG showed a normal heart. I knew then that the healing was done!

Friday morning, a heart catherization was done. That report too showed a normal heart with no damage—not even scarring! So positive was my healing that the doctor said: "It is as though you never had a heart attack!"

I thank God for the prayers of God's people and for His healing touch!

CHAPTER FORTY-ONE

Everett's Miracle!

by Faith Spears

At a Youth Camp in the Mississippi District in 1968, God filled a young camper, Everett Price, with the Holy Ghost.

Many years passed, and the same evangelist who was preaching that youth camp became Everett's pastor. By this time God had blessed Everett with a beautiful wife, Wanda, who shared his love of God's work. Into this family, in due time were born three lively, healthy sons. Everett was the song leader and Sunday School Superintendent, and he faithfully lived for Jesus. In a time when jobs were running out, God was good to allow Everett's work to continue. Along the way were decisions, opportunities to move away. . .but in the will of God; the Prices felt to stay home.

In the early spring of 1984, many times Everett became so ill while leading the songs that he had to go out and get some fresh air. . .or even to vomit. Slowly his face became swollen much of the time. Although he still was able to work, his boss often allowed him to stay in the office and do easier work.

After Everett had many tests and had visited different hospitals, Dr. John D. Bower, Professor of Medicine, Division of Nephrology at the University of Mississippi Medical Center diagnosed Everett's condition as Nephrotic Syndrome. This meant that the protein from his body was spilling out through his kidneys at the rate of 9.2 gr per twenty-four hours. The doctor said that was 1,000 times too much.

Some medication could be taken, but with very serious side effects, and then it was only one chance out of ten that it would even help. Eventually there would be kidney failure, then a kidney machine and hopefully a transplant.

The doctor's exact words to Everett were, "If a higher power doesn't intervene, it is a machine or a transplant."

During this time, prayer was offered, both in his home church, Powell's Grove, Mississippi, and at his mother's home church.

Everett was placed on the medication called Prednisone, 60 ml per day. He had to take different pills in order to sleep, and the side effects were awesome. Monthly he went to see what the progress was.

Letters signed by his physicians, starting in August of 1984, show that each month the rate of protein dropped. The last letter, dated April 2, 1985, states that there had been no deterioration of the kidney function and the protein was down to .33 gr per twenty-four hours. The doctor stated that the disease was in remission.

"It is a miracle!" No more pills! No kidney machine!

No transplant! Everett leads the singing like never before. It seems that one of his favorite songs is "My thanks to Him," which he sings often, hands raised, tears flowing.

He is able to work and to carry on the normal life of any thirty-year-old man. And it is all because of Calvary. Praise the Lord!

CHAPTER FORTY-TWO

God Still Answers "Hannah's" Prayer

by Raymond and Marlene McLanrin

What a mighty God we serve! In the next few sentences you will surely see that He is mighty for He can make that which is impossible possible.

After nine years of marriage and no children, my husband and I became concerned as to whether we would ever have any children. We agreed that I would visit a well-known gynecologist in the city at that time, Dr. Kenneth Von Pohle. After a series of tests he revealed to us his conclusions that we would never have any children.

Dr. Von Pohle encouraged us to consider adoption. He offered his aid in helping us to find a baby. We both wanted our own children so badly that we just could not seriously consider adoption.

One Sunday night after church service, we decided to ask our pastor, Reverend C. L. Dees to anoint us and pray for us that we would have children. An instant and very knowledgeable healing took place.

Within the following year our first child was born, a blonde, blue-eyed boy. We were so thrilled over this baby that we never thought about having a second child. Twenty-three months later along came another baby, this time a beautiful little girl. What more could we have asked for? God gave us a boy first and then a girl. Both children have been a blessing to us and have brought a world of joy to our home. For this we are thankful.

The McLanrin children.

CHAPTER FORTY-THREE

We Believe In Miracles

by Gil and Bobbie Richards

After seven years of marriage and infertility, God blessed us with our family. Our prayers were always, "Lord, if you give us a child, we will dedicate it back to You." He knew the desire of our hearts, but it was in *His* time and not *our* time that He had plans.

In 1977, our daughter, Jennifer, was born. Our gynecologist referred to her as "a miracle baby." Twenty-two months later we received a double portion and our unexpected second child, Lynn, was born. These children were dedicated to the Lord. We were thankful to have a family.

When Jennifer was two and a half and Lynn eleven months, we realized the importance of those dedication ceremonies—where couples put their trust in the Lord to watch over, bless and protect their children until they are at an age to find salvation for themselves. We felt that God would bless them mentally, physically and spiritually.

One evening during the girls' bath, the telephone rang and I rushed to answer it. It was one of the grandparents. I told her I would have to call her back.

Within a minute and a half I returned to the bathroom to find the oldest girl holding Lynn's face under water. I grabbed the baby and felt a cold lifeless body. I cried, "Jesus," and ran to her daddy, who came in. Calmly but quickly he laid Lynn on the carpet and began the CPR technique. I had "a little talk with Jesus" and He "made everything right."

By the time the paramedics and emergency teams arrived, our baby was breathing on her own. Life Flight attendants asked me to come along and have her admitted so that they could pump the water out of her stomach.

At approximately 8:00 p.m. little Lynn was on monitors and tubes. She was observed for brain damage. I learned that a baby can drown in only twenty seconds due to panicking and swallowing water so rapidly. I held my child in my arms and rocked her with tears in my eyes and a prayer in my heart. Down the hall was a four-year-old who had fallen into a pool the same day. I heard his mother scream when the doctors told her that her child had suffered extensive brain damage.

Around midnight Lynn opened her eyes and weakly cried "Mommy." Only God knows the joy and thanks I felt in my heart. The doctor had told me earlier that she would regain consciousness within eight hours if no brain damage had occurred. It had only been a little over four hours. To God be the glory!

The following year we were blessed with a third baby daughter, Julie. Three in five years! Doesn't God do all things well?

In August, 1983, another crisis came upon one of our children. This time our oldest, Jenny, had been sick for several days and had not been able to keep anything down. She was treated for viral symptoms, but suddenly jaundice set in and she had to be admitted to the hospital. She was diagnosed with a rare kidney disease called Hemolytic Uremic Syndrome. Her kidneys were down to 10% filtering and an emergency blood transfusion was set up. We were told that the kidneys were so destroyed that they might not be able to filter the "new blood" with only 10% usage. We were advised to look for an outside donor and keep family kidneys for reoccurrence of this disease.

We were heartbroken and very worried about her not accepting the blood. Then our pastor, Brother Paul Welch, walked in. Seeing the looks of dismay on our faces, he walked straight to Jenny and prayed, "Lord, let her accept this blood. Lord, You cleanse it and bless it. In the name of Jesus!"

That night Jenny sat up in bed and weakly said, "I'm hungry." The first time in eight days! Immediately she began improving and in three days her kidneys were up to 52% functioning. The specialists that were called in were amazed. They had only seen about three cases of this disease, and all of them lost all ability to function, requiring dialysis and later transplants.

As Jenny was discharged, we were informed not to expect over 52% usage of her kidneys because of such severe damage. We took the forty-two pound five-year-old home.

About six months later, a physical examination was required by our insurance company. An input/output comparison was done and analyzed at 94% functioning! Jenny is now seven years old, sixty-two pounds and doing great!

Our middle daughter, Lynn, is now five and has just concluded kindergarten and didn't make under a "B" on her report card for the entire year. Our third child, Julie, is three and a perfect picture of health. Thank you, Lord, for them.

Yes, we believe in miracles!

Lt. to Rt. Jennifer, Lynn, and Julie.

CHAPTER FORTY-FOUR

One of My Miracles

by Faith Spears

"You do all you can do out here. . .and we will do the same in the operating room. It is now impossible to save the baby, and the mother's life is also in danger."

It was January, 1951 in St. Francis Hospital, Monroe, Louisiana. Dr. Varino had just left the waiting room with these words. He didn't have to go into detail. . .my husband knew what he meant. So, he knelt to pray after calling my parents in Indiana to inform them of the great need for help in prayer. He stayed there until the doctor tapped him on the shoulder and said, "You have a son and the mother is going to make it also."

Steve was about two months premature, without fingernails, toenails, eyelashes, very small and weak, but he was doing good in the incubator.

We had saved the money for the doctor and hospital bills and had even tried to pay some along, but the doctor always said to wait. When we went to be released, we once again brought up the subject.

The doctor looked at all our charts and said, "I notice here that both your fathers are pastors, and so are you. Now I've made it a practice never to charge 'men of the cloth' and since it looks like we have another little preacher, I won't start now."

He told us that really the situation was totally beyond him, and according to medical knowledge, it was not possible for the baby to be alive as his oxygen supply was cut off before birth.

Yet, here we were, taking him home from the hospital!

Years have passed, and the doctor truly spoke the truth, because God did call Steve to preach. He has preached all around the United States and in many foreign countries.

CHAPTER FORTY-FIVE

Faith From God

by Martha Sparks, R.N.

The second doctor opened the exam room door and looked at my son, Robbie. The first doctor looked at the second. "Put him in?" The second doctor nodded his head and closed the door.

Someone called Children's Hospital and made the arrangements. I called my husband to let him know and was surprised to hear my voice tremble. Intellectually I had considered it, but emotionally I wasn't expecting it. My third son—five months old. The other two had never been sick.

I had known when I awoke that morning and checked him that he needed more treatment than I could provide. When he attempted to breathe in, his chest didn't expand. Instead, it looked as though his breastbone would touch his backbone—sternal retractions. Respiratory distress leading to lack of oxygenation leading to. . . . So I had called the pediatrician's office and made an appointment.

Antibiotics and humidified oxygen would have been fine, but hospitalization? Thoughts raced through my mind. "As soon as I get there, I'll call the church and request prayer. The hospital isn't far from the church; perhaps the pastor can come over. The church isn't much out of the way from here to the hospital. I'll drive by on the way."

When I reached the church a few minutes later, the doors were unlocked. As I had hoped, the pastor was in; he was downstairs working in the printing room. There was nothing impressive about the appearance: a church basement, a man in work clothes with ink on his hands, a small bottle of oil. Yet when he anointed Robbie and prayed for him, it was as though a vial of faith broke on top of my head and flowed over my entire body.

Robbie's condition did not change. I *knew* everything was all right. It seemed paradoxical. But there was no doubt in my mind.

I proceeded to the hospital. (Although now I don't know why I went; it didn't occur to me to do anything else.) We went through admissions and medical students accompanied us to the nursing unit.

"How long will he probably be in?"

"Five days."

Again I was surprised. Overnight had become acceptable, but five days! I still knew everything was fine.

Robbie was tucked into a crib with humidified oxygen, given an injection, some oral medication and fluids. Two medical students did histories and physicals on him. I did not object. I knew they needed the practice.

I left briefly to get something to drink. When I returned, the pediatric resident physician had drawn blood.

I had hand carried the pediatrician's orders to the hospital and knew he had not ordered blood work. The resident wanted to (insisted on) starting intravenous fluids. Again, the pediatrician had not ordered it. I didn't want to see Robbie restrained and unable to be held. I believe love is powerful medicine. Anyway, I knew everything was all right. I refused to have the IV started.

The resident physician argued saying Robbie could stop breathing anytime. Intellectually, I knew that. I could tell by watching him breathe and I knew the pediatrician had ordered an ENT (ear, nose and throat) specialist to consult, in case a tracheotomy had to be done. Yet faith saw other facts. God does not lie. Robbie would be fine.

The resident used a few more unpleasant tactics. I still refused the IV. He finally left. I thought, "What if I made the wrong decision? Maybe I should call my husband and ask him about it." But I knew the vial had not been broken on his head. He didn't know everything was fine. If he told me to go ahead, I couldn't disobey. Yet, I knew it wasn't necessary. I didn't call.

Then Satan said, "And if he dies?"

The answer was immediate. "If he dies, heaven, in God's presence, awaits. Certainly in heaven he will be well. He will be healed. Perhaps God can take care of him better without my help. And I cannot let keeping Robbie be more important to me than trusting and resting in the Lord. Live or die, all is well."

The peace was beautiful.

I slept in a chair beside his crib. At 7:30 a.m. I called the pediatrician at home. (He had phone hours at that time each day.) It was a strange but rewarding conversation. When he came later that day, he affirmed that Robbie needed lots of fluids—*orally*. He also said Robbie was doing well enough not to be awakened at night for fluids.

That was a good day. I could see Robbie's improvement with my physical eyes. Sister Mary Wallace visited. Talking with her is always helpful. Robbie slept late. I didn't let the medical students wake him. I believe sleep, like love, is therapeutic. I knew that his healing would be "on this side of eternity." I knew that I could help God take care of him for a few more years.

The next morning, less than two days after his admission, he was released.

His healing has endured. The wonderful experience of faith, the knowledge that with God in control all is well, has remained vivid through the years.

The experience reminded me of a message my home pastor preached when I was young and was concerned about lack of faith. He said, "You need enough faith to do what you know to do, what you know is right."

Before I entered the church, that's all the faith I had. I did what I knew to do: "Call for the elders of the church; and let them pray over him, anointing him with oil in the name of the Lord" (James 5:14). I didn't have faith for anything else. But how freely God gives—both faith and healing!

CHAPTER FORTY-SIX

A Chain of Miracles

by Donna Brown

Tuesday, May 15, 1973, a beautiful six pound, fourteen ounce baby boy was born. God gave us this little pride and joy. Unfortunately, during birth Kevin Michael swallowed too much amniotic fluid and was retracting quite heavily. Therefore he required oxygen within minutes after birth.

Although the situation was frightening, it was wonderful to be able to call upon God right then and know He would hear and answer. Little did we realize, however, that God was preparing us for what lay ahead in the following weeks. This was to be the first link of the "Chain of Miracles."

Kevin was kept in a special nursery for several extra hours, under close observation. But God touched him. He was breathing well on his own and the retracting gradually diminished. At last, he was brought to my room on Wednesday afternoon.

It wasn't until Friday that I noticed five tiny sores on the inside of his lower lip. Some three hours later I found out our baby had herpes disease, commonly known as cold sores in adults. That didn't sound too alarming until the nurse told me, "In newborns it can be fatal." After explaining how newborns have no immunities, she said that herpes could lead to heart disorders, liver diseases, respiratory problems, and other things.

Am I ever thankful for a big God! Since herpes is contagious to other newborns, I was requested to keep Kevin in my room and care for him day and night, watching to see that he ran no fever and that his color remained good.

The doctor said that it would be necessary to take a spinal tap to see if the infection had spread through Kevin's body. She also mentioned that the infectious contagious disease specialist would be in early the following morning to examine him.

I immediately called the church where I knew service was in progress. Thanks be to the Lord for His people who know how to call upon His name!

When the doctor and specialist came the following morning, to their amazement three of the sores were completely gone and the other two were fading away. They had expected Kevin's mouth to be covered with sores by this time. The doctor was almost embarrassed that she had brought the specialist in. She turned to me as if in a plea for help, "Why, they don't even look like the same sores, do they?" By Sunday morning the sores were completely gone and the second link was added to "The Chain."

During Saturday night, however, Kevin had run a fever and continued to do so on Sunday—the day we were both scheduled to go home. Instead, Kevin was put in isolation. I went home without him. Only a mother who's been through that could know how I felt! It was a most difficult time. But the Lord gave me the undergirding strength of the Holy Ghost. I called our Pastor, Brother Guy Roam, who came and prayed for Kevin. His fever left and never returned during his entire hospital stay!

But the worst was yet to come. On Monday morning the doctor called to tell us that Kevin had spinal meningitis. It was indeed a shock. At first it seemed almost too much to bear—that our world just crumbled beneath us. But God's Word says that He will not allow us any more troubles than we can bear. Our minds went back to the few days before when God had intervened on Kevin's behalf. We knew God had touched him then; surely this was no harder for the Lord to do. Of course, we called our pastor and many of the saints were contacted, and they fasted and prayed. What would we do without each other!

Brother Roam came again to the hospital. After scrubbing-up and donning the special gown and gloves, he was admitted to the isolation nursery. He opened the door of the isolette where our precious son lay, anointed him with oil, and prayed the prayer of faith. We felt God's presence in a sweet and mighty way.

I talked briefly with the doctor and told her we were believing God for a miracle. With tears in her eyes, she looked at me and said, "I think you'll get one." And truly God gave us one, not just one, but a whole "Chain of Miracles."

The doctor told us they would need to take a spinal tap every day until they got three negative cultures in a row, and that it would require at least three weeks of treatment in the hospital. He also said it may take a week or so to get the first negative culture, since newborns do not normally respond well to antibiotics. But praise God, "He responds well to our prayers!" And this was no normal situation—it was in God's hands!

The very first day they took a culture, it came back negative—and so did the second—and the third! Praise the Lord! They stopped tapping. God had miraculously touched Kevin. We felt the third link fall into place.

It was on the sixth day that another problem occurred. It seemed Kevin's head was growing too fast, an indication that he had fluid on his brain. The doctors felt it should be tapped, but decided to first have the neurologist examine him. Well, prayers went up and God arrived before the neurologist! Kevin's head growth stabilized from that day, and his head was not tapped! The chain had lengthened again.

Three more days passed. Kevin had been eating well and gaining weight all along and was responding so superbly that they were considering allowing him to come home after two weeks instead of three.

We were thrilled and excited. But God wasn't finished. It was time for another miracle.

On Wednesday of the second week, just three days prior to his possible homecoming, Kevin began to sleep a little more and eat a little less than usual, and he wasn't quite as perky as he had been. On Friday, they gave him some heart x-rays and a brain-wave test.

The following day is one I'll never forget. My husband Lonnie left early that morning to join the church in our "March For Missions." He had been gone about three hours when the call came. Kevin had taken a tragic turn for the worse. He had a heart murmur and X-rays showed a heart disorder. But more serious, Kevin indicated a "very poor" on the brain-wave test. This signified that he'd been having brain seizures. When I asked if this meant he would be retarded, the doctor would only reply, "It's like I said, the pattern he indicates is very poor."

The doctors started him on seizure medication. They said he was too young to tell what damage was done, that all we could do was wait and watch him as he developed and grew older. We had already been told that 50% of the babies having this type of meningitis do not even live, 25% of the ones that do, have those residual effects. But the greater the need, the greater the miracle!

I must confess that I began to question myself. Was I trying too hard to hold onto my baby? Was I praying *against* God's will? I *knew* God was able to heal Kevin, but was that His plan? I had been thinking about the current SFC slogan, "The Evening Sacrifice." Though this may sound absurd, I even wondered if perhaps this was the sacrifice God required of us.

After some time in prayer, I told the Lord, just as sincerely as I knew how, "Lord, if it's Your will, take Kevin, but if it's Your will to let us keep him, then please heal him completely." Only the Lord knew until the time of this writing that I told Him if He desired Kevin back, that rather than people sending flowers, we would request memorial offerings which would be given to SFC. God knew I meant it from my heart.

When I finished praying, I did not know whether God would heal Kevin or take him, but I felt a peace that whatever happened would be God's will and I wanted that above all! I knew He knew best!

I felt I should notify my husband about the call, but I didn't want him to quit marching. I knew he would not want to. Being Youth Leader, he had spent many hours of preparation for this event, and, besides, it was for no personal gain. The march was to help souls hear the gospel!

I called Brother Roam and asked him to pray. He advised me to tell Lonnie right away. When I located him on the march and told him, he looked at me with his deep faith in God and said, "Honey, we'll just have to put it in the Lord's hands. He's already done so much; He'll take care of him. We'll pray as we march. Now don't worry!" Thank God for a God-loving husband!

Some six or seven hours later all the marchers had gathered back at the church for a dinner and service. It was a beautiful time of worship. During the service, Brother Roam told the people of our baby's critical turn, and asked for seven people to come forward to believe for Kevin's healing. During that prayer, we knew God touched Kevin and knew He was going to bring our baby through the ordeal. The service was highlighted by Brother J. D. Langford's outstanding message on the "Evening Sacrifice." God's presence made our heavy hearts glad!

At the close of the service our pastor asked my husband and me to come forward and asked everyone to gather around us and to pray that God would strengthen us. And surely He did! We walked out new people.

When we arrived home, we called the hospital to learn that Kevin had awakened at 9:00 p.m.—the same time we had been praying. And he wanted something to eat. This was the first time in three days that he awoke on his own and was ready to eat. And he continued to awaken every three to four hours from then on. And the chain continued.

An extensive series of heart tests revealed nothing wrong with the heart. They determined that the heart murmur was nothing serious—something that he would eventually outgrow.

Kevin contacted a type of bacterial virus. When a culture was made of it, it began growing out on a plate that normally only "bad bugs" grow out on. So Kevin was put back in isolation. But God moved again! The next day the culture had grown into something completely different—and not nearly so serious. That really puzzled the doctors. Kevin was taken out of isolation.

When three weeks finally passed, we brought Kevin home. What a glorious day! And God is still performing miracles in his life! By the time of Kevin's first check-up, the enlarged liver he'd had was down to a normal size. When his first two teeth came in, they had black streaks through them in front and back. According to the doctor, this was probably from the great amount of medicine administered during his illness. He also said that it is possible that all of Kevin's teeth may be the same. So I asked God to touch him—and He did! The black streaks are almost completely gone in the front and are leaving in the back! I can hardly wait to show the doctor. We're believing the Lord that all the other teeth will be perfectly white.

Next came a terrible skin infection. We applied no medicine at all—only prayer, and God did the work. Later

Kevin had an attack of bronchial asthma, with bronchial pneumonia. God gloriously brought him through.

And the latest "link" was added when we took Kevin in for his eight-month check-up. The same doctor who told me seven months before that Kevin would require seizure medication twice daily for years, said that we could discontinue one of the doses.

Our little "bundle of miracles" at nine months old weighed twenty-four pounds and was pleasant and lovable as could be; he was as rambunctious as any baby his age, crawling around getting into everything he could.

Kevin is now twelve years old, an honor student at New Life Christian School, and is filled with the Holy Ghost.

He participated in Junior Quizzing in 1981 and made the All-Star Team in 1983. He was the number one man in point average on that team. Today he has no known health problems.

To God be all the glory!

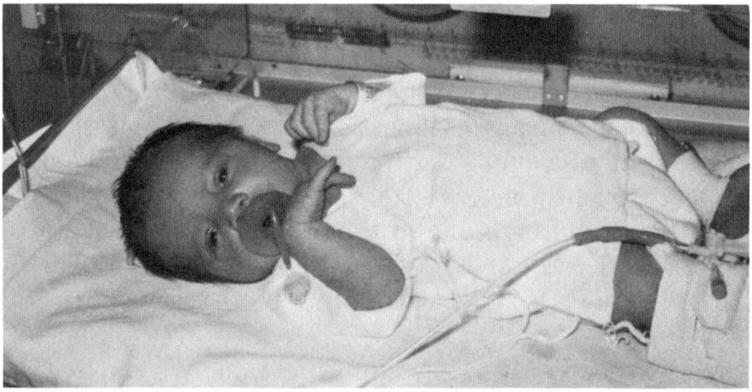

Kevin at one week

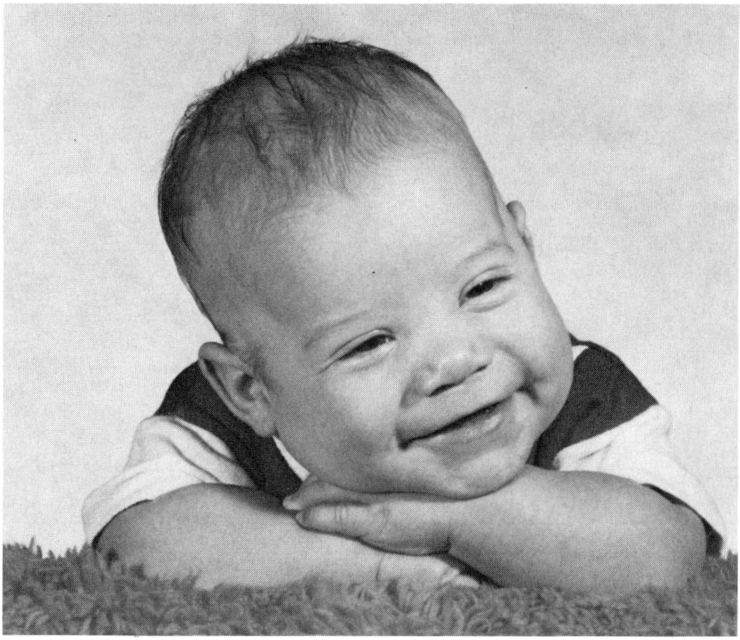

Kevin Brown at 3 months.

Kevin Brown, 10 years old.

Progress Report

School Year 1983 - 84

KEVIN BROWN
Student

FIFTH
Department

B. BINGHAM
Supervisor

New Life

New Life Christian School

Kevin's report card in 5th grade.

Name KEVIN BROWN Grade 5

A = excellent B = good C = average D = poor

F = failure S = satisfactory U = unsatisfactory

Grading period	1st	2nd	1st Sem.	3rd	4th	2nd Sem.
Math	A	A	A	A-	A	A
Lnaguage	A	A	A	B+	A	A-
History	A	A+	A+			
Science				A+	A+	A+
Spelling	A	A+	A	A	A+	A
Penmanship	B	B	B	B	B	B
Reading	B	A	A-	A-	B+	A-
Phonics						
Bible	A	A+	A	A	A+	A
Music	A	A	A	A	A	A
P.E.	S	S	S	S	S	S
Band	A-	A-	A-	A-	A-	A-

Grading period	1st	2nd	3rd	4th
Times tardy	0	0	1	0
Days absent	1½	1½	5	0
Scripture memory	[illegible]	[illegible]	[illegible]	[illegible]
Number of times homework was not completed	0	0	0	0

Parent signature

1. Lonnie B. Brown
2. Lonnie B. Brown
3. Lonnie B. Brown

Comments:

1 A Honor Roll 97%
2. A Honor Roll 98%
A Honor Roll 1st Sem.
3 A Honor Roll 97%
4 A Honor Roll
A Honor Roll 2nd Sem.

Kevin, I have enjoyed having you in my class. Keep up the great work.
Sis. Bingham

CHAPTER FORTY-SEVEN

Memories

by Ruby Cox

"Lizzie, we have come today to tell you and Orville that unless you call a doctor today for your baby, we are going to call and report you to the county authorities!" The three grim-faced neighbors, lifelong friends of the Sampson family, seated themselves in the front room, announced their threat and meant every word.

Lizzie was a young nurse-midwife who always responded to the community's calls for help—to birth a baby or to nurse a child sick with whooping cough or diphtheria or to locate a doctor in an emergency for a situation she could not handle.

Many times Lizzie had visited the homes of these same three neighbors and given tender, loving care to their sick and dying loved ones.

But this time Lizzie had gone too far in her newfangled religion, or so the neighbors thought, not calling the doctor for her dying baby and believing God for her healing.

She and Orville, recent converts to the Pentecostal way, and excited with the new truths, were indeed trusting God in all things as the Bible commanded and as the preacher taught.

And then the test of faith: Frances, their three year old baby, had a growth the size of an orange suddenly appear behind her right ear. As the days passed, she grew listless and steadily weaker as high fever raged through her tiny frame.

Lizzie and Orville, the young parents, took turns rocking her, praying and sending for the preacher and elders to help them pray.

But Frances' condition only worsened. Lizzie held her dying baby, looking into a once elfish face, now pale and wan from the sickness. She saw the strawberry blonde hair curling around her forehead and the dark curly eyelashes closed over her beautiful blue eyes. Tears silently rolled down the mother's face.

Lizzie mentally re-lived the precious little one's short life—the birth, the goo's and burbles, the first step, the first word. She seemed to remember all the cute little sayings, all the words Frances had mispronounced, but how smart and pert she seemed to be. Frances certainly was joy, a little spark, to all the family.

But now Lizzie faced the toughest moment of her life; to lose a child was indeed a trial to her new found faith. Her emotions fought against her knowledge and her carnal thinking battled her spiritual mind; should she call a doctor or should she continue to trust in God? As she settled it in her heart, she softly whispered, "Dear Jesus, our heavenly Father, we gave our children to You to do with as it pleases you."

The three neighbors sat silently, waiting for a word of decision from the parents.

Frances lay on a bed in the same room. It was a few tense minutes. Finally Orville said, "Let's pray one more time, Mama." They knelt, one on each side of the bed, and reaching across the baby, they clasped hands.

Oh! What a prayer! The utterings came straight from the very core of their soul.

Orville prayed first, tears streaming down his cheeks. Only the angels in heaven could describe the beauty and simplicity of that prayer.

The neighbors sat uneasily in their chairs just a few feet away.

Then Lizzie prayed, her mother's heart desperately reaching out to a never-failing God for her precious bundle of joy whose life was hanging by a mere thread. While she was still praying, Frances raised up from the bed. In plain view of the three neighbors, the growth started shrinking until it disappeared completely.

Then a tiny voice piped out, "Mama, I'm hungry."

"Of course, you are hungry. What would you like to eat?"

"Cornbread and milk."

The young father picked up his little daughter and danced around the room rejoicing, "Thank You, Jesus. Thank You, Jesus!"

The three neighbors with wide-eyed stares silently tiptoed to the door and left the house.

"Yea, though I walk through the valley and shadow of death I will fear no evil for thou art with

me . . . thou preparest a table before me in the presence of mine enemies . . . surely goodness and mercy shall follow me all the days of my life and I shall dwell in the house of the Lord forever. Amen."

CHAPTER FORTY-EIGHT

The Echo of Little Footsteps

by Libby Fink

Thud thud...thud thud...thud thud. The thud of the revolving door did not seem to detract Emma Jane's reflections of the past few days as she briskly scurried down the sidewalk. Children seemed to be the prominent attraction as her eyes skimmed the sidewalks. It was only a few days before that her daughter Becky was playing with other children, but now she lay motionless.

Time also seemed to be motionless. How much longer could it possibly be before the physicians brought back the test results? Becky had been ill for two days then her temperature had shot up while her mother was working. Grandma Thomas had packed her in ice, but the fever had not diminished. A phone call at work told Emma Jane the tragic message. Becky was paralyzed from her neck down.

The silence in the waiting room was suddenly pierced. "Mrs. LeRoux?" Emma Jane responded, "Yes. That's me! How is my daughter?"

The physician looked down at the floor, reluctant to inform the young mother of the tragic news. Then his eyes met hers once again. "I need to talk with you in another room, please."

When they were alone he said, "We have run some tests on your daughter. She has Aseptic Meningitis. This is similar to polio. If she lives. . . ." He paused and then repeated, "If she lives, she will remain paralyzed the rest of her life. Asceptic Meningitis victims often have convulsions and remain in the position that they have thrown themselves into for life. Your daughter has not had one of these yet. But she remains paralyzed from her neck down."

Emma Jane returned to her parents and informed them of the test results. Saddened by the news, they once again called on their Creator. He was the God who created the universe. He spoke the world into existence. He could heal their granddaughter.

Quickly Emma Jane made the second call to her pastor. After hearing the results of the tests, Reverend Oliver Spencer called a prayer and fast on Becky's behalf. The physicians could not cure Becky; even though it was the late 50's there had not been a cure developed.

When Emma Jane had brought her paralyzed baby to the hospital, but the doctor could offer no hope, Emma Jane knew God, who had given a dead man life, healed a deaf man, and restored a blind man's vision.

The next day she was only allowed to look through a window at Becky, who was in the isolation ward. Peering through the window, tears streaming down her face, she felt helpless. She could see Becky's delicate form. Her beautiful brown hair was a touching frame to her angelic face. How could such a thing happen to an innocent child as this?

The isolation sign and the walls served as a barricade, but she could at least see her daughter. Before she left, Emma Jane once again prayed for God to heal Becky.

Visiting hours were over, but Becky had one Visitor who came to see her that night. Near the bed of the petite four-year-old girl was a brilliant light that consumed the darkness of the room. When it left, Becky was healed.

It was a new day in Becky's life. When she woke up, she sat up in bed. The child had fallen asleep an invalid, but she awoke a healthy child. The child who was paralyzed now had to be restrained in bed for additional tests.

Knowing nothing of the miracle of healing, Emma Jane left work to go immediately to the hospital. To her amazement, Becky was sitting up in bed and moving around! Emma Jane ran to the elevator, went to the gift shop and searched through the gifts until she found a small doll.

Returning to the isolation ward, she slipped in, kissed and hugged Becky, and put the doll in her arms.

The physician informed Emma Jane of the news. "We have taken additional spinal taps and blood work. We can no longer find any trace of Asceptic Meningitis! Earlier this morning, a man who claims to be your pastor visited Becky and said that she was healed."

As we were leaving the hospital, Becky jumped from the wheelchair and raced to meet Grandpa Thomas. The physician, who had accompanied us down the elevator, heard a lady complaining about the young girl running through the hospital. He turned to the lady, pointed to the nurse and the mother who were both crying and then to the child and the grandfather. With tears in his eyes he said, "Lady, you have just seen a miracle! That child came through those doors paralyzed earlier this week. We could do nothing for her, but God healed her. She is the only one with the disease to be healed and to walk out of this hospital. You would run too! She can run and play with the other children again!"

Lt. to Rt. Dave, Jim, Becky, and Ann LeRoux.

CHAPTER FORTY-NINE

Miracle Boy

by Reverend and Mrs. Walter Droke

Our miracle began to develop in the latter part of 1981. My husband, Walter Droke, and I became concerned about our third child, thirteen-month-old Eric Walter. At first it seemed simple enough to give Eric a little antacid to eliminate the more-than-usual offensive odor of his burp. But gradually even that did not work. Our concern grew.

In December of 1981 our church had a wonderful revival with Sister Louise Potter from Martinsville, Indiana. We requested Pastor Denzil Richardson to anoint our son with oil and pray for his healing in Jesus' name. The Lord heard our prayer and we felt that everything would be all right.

Eric continued to grow worse, however. I would have to hold him away from me and turn my head to keep from being nauseated when he burped. He also began vomiting every evening. We could almost set our watch at 6:00 p.m.

to expect it any minute. At times he would seem to feel fine and the odor would not be so offensive after he vomited. But one night as we were cleaning up after he vomited, my husband realized that the large pieces of undigested green beans had been in Eric's stomach for more than forty-eight hours. We called the pediatrician.

Although two pediatricians had told us on several occasions that there was nothing to worry about, Dr. Miller told us to enter Eric in the Pediatric Clinic in Jackson, Tennessee, the next morning for observation and tests.

On February 15, 1982, Dr. James Roy Appleton, Jr., urologist, performed surgery on Eric on the possibility of some glands being wrapped around his intestines. Finding no interference with his intestines, the doctor removed the appendix. Eric went home in a few days.

The day after we arrived home, Eric's vomiting reoccurred and we returned to the Pediatric Clinic.

We were referred to a Pediatric Gastrointerologist at LeBonheur Hospital in Memphis, Tennessee. When we went for Eric's appointment with Dr. Peter Whitington, they left us in a small room to wait. To this day I believe the Lord sent some kind of sleeping gas into that little room. Immediately Walter and I became very sleepy and Eric, laying across my lap, fell into a sound sleep. When Dr. Whitington came in, he told us of the different tests they would begin that afternoon. Eric slept on. As Dr. Whitington rose to leave, he reached over and pulled up Eric's gown to examine his stomach. We saw a big knot roll from one side of Eric's abdomen to the other and back. Medical students were brought in to observe his "Most pronounced example of trapped gases due to upper gastrointestinal blockage I've ever seen!"

Most of the tests were eliminated. They told us that a thin membrane could have developed at the exit to Eric's stomach and they just might be able to "pull the plug" when they went down his esophagus with an endoscopic light to look around in his stomach. That would mean we could go home the next day.

After the surgery, the doctor was not optimistic. "I'm sorry, I don't have good news. Your little boy is very sick." He proceeded to tell us that Eric had one of four things wrong with him. One was a disease which could possibly be cured with several months' hospitalization. Second was a disease which was treatable but not curable. Third was ulcers—which he ruled out because Eric did not complain of pain. Fourth was cancer. In any event we were to be prepared for a hospital stay of several weeks and possibly several months. Six biopsies had been taken of Eric's stomach lining and Dr. Whitington told us he would tell us which of the four diagnosis was correct as soon as he received the laboratory report the next morning.

Neither of us could say anything as the doctor left the room. But as Walter and I walked to the window almost in shock, we knew where to turn. Looking into the blue sky, we began to call on the name of our Lord Jesus. And into that room flowed a presence bringing strength, comfort and peace. We committed our son into His care. People of our church were called and prayer was offered again.

It seemed the night would never pass. Morning brought us no word from Eric's doctor. Noon came, then 2:00 p.m., 4:00 p.m., but Dr. Whitington still had not come. Finally about 6:00 p.m. Dr. Whitington entered the room. "Well, I'm sorry I'm late, but I just couldn't believe the lab report I received this morning. So I went down to look at the slides myself! I *know* what I saw when I looked into Eric's stomach. There was a lot of red, angry tissue, and so much infection that I couldn't even see where the opening was supposed to be. But the tissue at the lab shows no sign of infection. It's perfectly normal stomach tissue! I just don't understand it!"

But we knew that God had answered our prayers. Dr. Wren did a simple surgery on Eric's stomach to make an opening where it had been closed off by the excess tissue. We took him home after only five days!

It was not until later that we heard through a friend who worked at LeBonheur that the lab people and others were referring to our Eric as the "Miracle Boy."

Eric is now four years old and going strong. He's never had another minute's trouble with his stomach (except to keep it full!). Our thanks to God for answering our prayers.

CHAPTER FIFTY

Just In Time

by Fred E. Kinzie

It seemed my feet wouldn't go fast enough! I was headed for the prayer room, desperately anxious to get there!

I was confused and sorely perplexed! I needed an answer. Two of my most trusted friends, both fellow ministers, had given me conflicting advice. They were both older than myself with many years of experience handling pastoral problems. Why hadn't they talked with the same voice? I was as torn now as before soliciting their help!

One had said to turn to the law and get its help before that individual drives you crazy. The other had said, "Oh Brother Kinzie, whatever you do, don't do that!"

I had listened to the second voice. It had seemed the easy way to go. But it had not worked, no problem had been solved and I was in a desperate state of mind as of this very moment.

I had rolled and tossed all night long with the problem confronting me. I tried to convince myself that I really didn't have a problem, but it was ever before me regardless of how I tried to erase it.

Just before dawn that morning I reasoned with myself that I had followed the second voice and it had not worked. Why not look at the first voice again? I determined the first thing I'd do when I arose in the morning was to call my lawyer and take whatever steps he'd suggest.

As soon as I thought he'd be in his office, I called. His secretary answered saying he wasn't in yet but would be shortly. Should he call back? "No," I answered, "I'll not be at this phone. I'll call a little later!"

I left the house and headed for my office at the church. "This whole thing is silly," I said to myself as I walked. "Why don't I just go to the prayer room and pray this thing through? God has the answer! My friends mean well and have my welfare at heart, but they're not living in my shoes. They see everything in the light of their experiences. I have to pray this one through for myself!"

With that determination, I quickened my steps and hurried on to the church. I headed right to the prayer room and dropped on my knees. It didn't take long to get into the spirit of earnest prayer.

I could not have been on my knees more than a couple of minutes, praying earnestly, when a verse of Scripture crossed my mind. I tried to erase it, thinking it an obstruction from Satan to get me away from prayer. Then it came again! I ignored it a second time, praying over it or at least trying to pray over it. But I couldn't! It was not the text of the Scripture, but just its place in the Bible. "If God were speaking to me, He'd use the text, not its position in the Bible!" I reasoned. The Scripture reference was I Kings 15:22.

Finally, when praying had been distracted to the point I couldn't concentrate, I decided it was foolish to allow something this silly to keep me from praying. I'd get my Bible, read the verse of Scripture—it would be something so far removed from the point, something very foolish—then I could get down to the business at hand and touch God and get my answer from Him!

Finding my Bible, I turned to the verse of Scripture and read it. I discovered it was the key verse in a story about Asa, a king of Judah. I read and reread the story. Asa had turned to outside help in hiring Benhadad, king of Syria to help him in his battle with Baasha, king of Israel. When Benhadad turned his army against Israel in the north, Baasha had to pull back his forces in the south where he had been fighting against Asa. This gave Asa back his territory in the south and the war was over. It had been the right thing for Asa to do, and God had honored it, giving him rest from his enemies. *This was my answer!*

"Why had I not taken this course earlier?" I asked myself. This had to be God's answer to my problem. The step I had taken this morning was the right one, and all I needed to do now was follow it up with a return call to my lawyer!

Although it seemed I had the answer, I still felt a little uneasy. Maybe I should read a little further. I reread the story, but found nothing that changed anything. I was just about to head for the telephone and call my lawyer when I noticed a *pp. 2 Chronicles 16:12* in the margin of my Bible. That meant there was a similar account of this in II Chronicles. I turned to it and read the whole story there. Was I ever glad I read that account.

It was essentially the same with one exception. This record told about God's anger being stirred up at Asa for turning to outside help instead of to Him. He pointed out a similar incident where Asa had trusted the Lord and He brought him out victoriously. Why had he now turned to someone else?

A judgment was pronounced upon him for doing this. He would have nothing but wars from here on out!

W-H-E-W! II Chronicles changed the whole picture for me. Supposing I go ahead and hire the lawyer? I would not be trusting God. Since the Lord had called this to my attention, is it possible that wars would follow me then, too? Instead of solving my problem I would be adding to them!

The sweet presence of the Lord swept over me as I thanked Him for this timely answer to prayer. My answer was to simply *Trust Him!*

About that time, the phone rang in my office. I hurried back and found my lawyer on the phone. "Reverend Kinzie," he said, "my secretary said you called this morning. Is there something I can do for you?"

"Sir," I answered back triumphantly, "I have my answer. Between the time I called you and now I found the direction I am to go. No, everything is all right, but I do appreciate your calling back!" He had never called me back like this! I usually always had to run him down. "Isn't this just like Satan to try to confuse me?" I thought.

Replacing the receiver on the hook, I walked away from the phone with an assurance in my heart that God had everything under control and that in His own good time, He would handle the whole situation just right.

"And," you ask, "did it work out that way?"

Did it ever! A minister, Brother Tom Fred Tenney, came a few weeks later to preach weekend services for us. Without his knowing anything about the situation, two outstanding, anointed sermons he preached brought victory to the church, and actually solved the problem.

Thank God for His answer to prayer, His way, not mine!

CHAPTER FIFTY-ONE

A Lesson In Counseling

by Rev. C. R. Duke

We had some people in great difficulty who came to me for counsel. As they told their story, I was moved of God to tell them God would give the answer by the next Sunday morning, which was one week.

They were quick to accept this and went away knowing for sure it would come to pass. As the week progressed, I prayed but no answer came. By Wednesday my faith was growing small, but again we assured them that God was going to give us the answer by Friday. I was surely praying.

On Friday I needed to go to another town. As I drove along my mind was completely taken up by this need. Suddenly as I approached a bridge there was an old man standing along side the road. He did not appear to want a ride, however, I felt I should pick him up. But this was against my natural feeling as I never pick up anyone on the road. Since he did not appear to be wanting a ride,

I drove by, but a deep sense moved over me to stop, so I did.

I had to back up as I had driven by. Apparently he was just not interested as he did not even offer to open the door. So I opened the door and asked if he needed a ride. He did not say a word, but he did get in.

I made small talk about the weather. He did not say one word and I just thought I had picked up a dud, so I just let my mind move back to my problems.

Suddenly he said he had some children in trouble and he had come to bring them help. Then he discussed their problem which was the same as my problem. I listened very carefully. Then I asked what he was going to tell them. As he talked, I knew this was what I would tell my people as this was exactly what they needed. Then he simply said, "I will get out here."

I pulled into a small service station and he got out. I felt so good about his advice that I thought I would buy his dinner. I reached into my pocket to get the money out and told him to wait so I could give him the money. He bent down and looked back at me. "I have meat to eat that you know not of."

As I drove off it hit me what he said. I looked back but did not see him. Through him Jesus had given me the answer to the problem, but the man's identity has made me wonder who he was. Perhaps one of God's angels.

CHAPTER FIFTY-TWO

A Move Of God

by Mrs. A. H. Browning

In the summer of 1952 the Texico District was having one of its first district-wide camp meetings in Palo Dura Canyon south of Amarillo, Texas. Brother C. A. Nelson was the camp evangelist. One night Brother Nelson preached about Jesus taking Barabbas' place by dying on the cross. All at once he stopped in mid-sentence All the men on the platform instantly stood to their feet, looking intently back toward the congregation. Almost to a person, the audience rose to their feet, some swaying to and fro, some running from the tabernacle.

A ten-year-old boy had thrown a handful of gravel upon the roof of the tabernacle. But it was more than just that. Most did not hear the sound of the gravel but sensed rather, a strong presence of God. Brother Browning and I saw something seemingly coming from the Lord, coming from the north, sweeping over the people. People began to cry and pray. Saints and ministers were outside the tabernacle with upraised hands asking God to forgive their sins and neglect. People were asking each others forgiveness and making things right. The Lord seemed to flash everything we had been doing wrong on the screens of our minds. After we sought God for a while, Brother Nelson resumed his sermon just where he had been interrupted. Perfect quiet rested on the congregation.

After the service we gathered at the dining hall for fellowship. No one seemed to be too hungry; rather we discussed the unusual service. All at once a deep burden fell on my soul and I began to run around inside the dining hall screaming. All that were gathered fell on their faces and began to pray. After much stirring prayer, a message came through in tongues that one of our missionaries, Jean Bailey, was at the point of death. We found out later that she had been wading a river in the jungle and had contacted some kind of poison in her foot and that she had received healing that very night. Almost everyone prayed all night long and what a prayer meeting it was!

We had a glorious service the next morning. The Lord seemed to lay a powerful testimony upon me. Some lady asked forgiveness for cutting her little girl's hair. Another lady asked that I pray for her little girl who had every symptom of polio. The child's name was Kathy Chandler. This little girl, who is now Kathy Gilmer and the mother of several beautiful children, came to me at our recent conference in Anaheim, California and asked me if I remembered her. I told her I would never forget her as she was the young lady I had prayed for at the Canyon camp meeting. She verified the fact that she had been completely healed.

It is rather strange how God chooses to work. A little boy thoughtlessly throws a handful of gravel. God uses that to stir and convict a large group of people, bring them to their knees in repentance and confession and causing them to pray all night and to touch Him for people halfway around the world.

CHAPTER FIFTY-THREE

God's Strange Way Of Answering Prayer

By *Mrs. A. H. Browning*

In 1935 when we were pastors of a church in Menard, Texas, we received a call from Abilene, Texas, from a brother-in-law informing us that my two-year-old nephew was gravely ill and they had been unable to get victory for him. They asked us to come and pray.

We started out in our Model—A Ford for Abilene. For days heavy rain poured down. We came to a place where the roadway was covered with water almost as far as we could see. We had passed a flagman in a small town, but for some reason he failed to stop us and explain the road situation. In the name of the Lord we eased into the water and slowly drove across. The car did not falter or get drowned out.

Later we came to a place where the highway was completely barricaded with roads leading to the right and left. We just took the road which seemed right to us and made it through without any trouble.

We arrived in Abilene in the late afternoon. Immediately we went to prayer and continued praying well into the next day. The heavens seemed like brass and the child grew no better. Finally, the father of the boy said to us, "I'm the one who really needs prayer." So we turned our efforts in his behalf. When the father made everything right with the Lord, the little boy was instantly healed. God has many mysterious ways in which He works.

CHAPTER FIFTY-FOUR

Healing And Salvation

By Martha Sparks, R.N.

I have heard my mother tell how her parents came to know the Lord.

She was about two. One day she fell off the bed and landed on her head. After that she began to have infrequent, but severe, spasms. They took her to a doctor. He only said, "They'll get more and more frequent until she dies."

Grandpa had heard about a tent revival where they prayed for the sick. He suggested to Grandma that they take Mom to be prayed for.

Hands were laid on in the name of Jesus. Mom is now seventy-six years old. After she was prayed for, there were no more spasms.

My grandparents realized God's healing power and soon came to know his saving power as well.

There are many children, grandchildren, great-grandchildren and great-great-grandchildren who know the Lord because of that fall-illness-healing years ago.

CHAPTER FIFTY-FIVE

God Brought Richard Back To Life!

by Reverend & Mrs. W. M. Parker

I humbly submit the following account of how God raised my son from the dead as a tribute to the mighty power of our Lord Jesus Christ.

On August 10, 1981, my nineteen-year-old son, Richard, and I were working on the church roof. Rick stepped backward off the roof, hitting the back of his head on a rafter and fell unconscious sixteen feet onto concrete.

I watched helplessly as he fell from the roof, about ten feet from me. As I gathered my son's body in my arms, there was no sign of life—no breathing or any sound of a heartbeat. There is no doubt in my mind that Rick was dead on impact. Many things flashed through my mind as I prayed. My wife and I had waited thirteen years for Richard, and when God gave him to us, we knew and openly acknowledged him as a "gift from God." We had spent our entire thirty-two years of married life walking with and working for God. I simply could not understand why God would take Rick back, twenty-one days before his twentieth birthday.

Even as I began to question God in my own mind, He impressed me with the verse of Scripture: "All things work together for good to those who love God and are called according to His purpose." I found my prayers changing, for I began to ask God humbly to have His own way! When my prayer changed, Rick instantly began to breathe and his heart began to beat again!

There are no words to express my feelings at that moment! I was humbly grateful, elated, and thrilled to the depths of my being. I knelt there on the concrete, holding my bleeding son's body in my arms, and praised my God for His mercy, kindness and boundless love!

Someone had called an emergency vehicle, and about the time Rick came back to life, it arrived. The paramedics took one look at Rick and called for the "Flight for Life" helicopter. The nurse and paramedics gently eased Rick onto a stretcher, after placing a neck brace on him, and quickly loaded him into the helicopter for flight to the hospital.

At this point everyone believed his back and neck were broken and that he had extensive internal injuries and brain damage. In flight to the hospital, Rick again lost all vital signs and for a few minutes he was apparently again dead. God restored him to life a *second* time. When he was wheeled into the emergency room at the hospital, he died on the table. God restored him to life a *third* time.

My wife soon arrived at the hospital. I have asked her to write the next segment of this story.

* * * * * *

It was Monday, August 10, a rainy, cold bleak day.

As I sat at my desk doing the usual Monday's chores, the church accounts, I heard my doorbell ringing over and over and someone pounding on my door! I rushed downstairs and opened the door. Standing there were two ladies from our church, both with ashen faces, telling me Rick had been taken to the hospital in the "Flight for Life" helicopter. I was cognizant of the fact that "Flight for Life" was used only in life or death situations and that the survival statistic was one out of every ten. I sent them back to the church to call everyone they knew and ask them to pray. Mike, my seventeen-year-old son, and I immediately left for the hospital.

Enroute, I felt that I had lost Rick. At first I thought, "Oh, God, please. I can't give up my son. You gave him to me!" God brought to my mind the fact that the "gift of life" comes only from Him, giving Him the irrevocable right to recall that gift whenever He sees fit. I asked God to forgive me and began praying with all my might that God would help me accept what I had to accept in the way He would have me accept it. Immediately I felt a sense of peace envelop me like a warm blanket!

When we reached the hospital, my husband met me at the door of the emergency room and told me that the hospital personnel believed Rick's neck and back were broken and that he had extensive internal injuries and brain damage. I saw the dreadful hurt in my husband's face as he told me that our son had died on impact with the concrete. I watched his countenance change to a painful question as he said, "But, God brought him back to life!"

I did not want to hear anything else: I was overwhelmed with an urgency to see my son and I became insistent in my demands to see him. My husband, our younger son, our youth minister, Brother French, and the emergency room attendant all held me back from going in the room to see Rick. Hearing all the commotion, the nurse came out of the room where Rick was and told me emphatically that I could not go in to Rick. I tried to explain to all of them the urgency I felt, but they could not seem to understand.

I finally went outside the hospital and stood by the door praying that God would open a way for me to get to Rick. The doctor who was working on Rick came outside and told me it was impossible, that all hospital rules forbade my seeing my son. I tried to explain to him, praying all the time that he would see the urgency of the situation. But he said over and over, "Please understand, Mrs. Parker, I cannot let you see Rick." Just as insistent, I replied over and over, "I do not understand—you don't understand—I must see my son—I MUST!"

After four attempts to make me say I understand, he finally walked away. I thought, "Oh God, I've failed. I don't even know why, but I *know* that I must see Rick!" I felt as though everything inside me was bleeding. I felt utter despair and completely alone!

Only about one minute passed before the nurse came hurrying out. "Mrs. Parker, we have waived all hospital rules and you can go in to see Rick for just one minute!" As I walked in, I saw Rick lying in a pool of his own blood on a table, blood gushing out his ear. He was not moving and his face was blue. The nurse said, "You can talk to him if you want to. He won't hear you—he is unconscious."

I walked over to him and placed my hand on his cheek

and said softly, "Rick, this is Mom." He immediately opened his eyes and said, "Mom, take the needle out of my arm. It hurts." Never has anything sounded more beautiful to my ears! The nurse and doctor seemed to fall back against the walls in absolute amazement. I said, "Rick, can you hear me?" He said, "Yes." I said, "Can you understand what I am saying?" He said, "Yes." I said, "Rick, people are praying for you in Jesus' name all over this country, and you are going to be all right."

I cannot explain how I knew he would be all right, but as soon as I touched him I *knew* he was going to be all right. He again opened his eyes and said, "Mom, are you sure?" I said, "Yes, Son, believe me, I'm sure!" He said, "OK!"

The doctor moved to my side. "Mrs. Parker, we are taking Rick for a CAT scan and will immediately take him into surgery. It is already set up and the neurosurgeon is waiting to operate on his brain. He has extensive damage."

I answered, "Do whatever you feel must be done, but believe me, doctor, Rick is going to be all right." He took a step back, obviously, thinking, "That lady is crazy!"

By the time they wheeled Rick to the elevator to take him for the CAT scan, approximately two or three minutes had passed and his face had color again. He was conscious and talked with his dad, his brother, and Brother French.

A few minutes later the nurse came rushing in. "I know I'm not supposed to tell you, but I've just got to—Rick does not have to have brain surgery! His brain is not damaged as we believed, only shaken and bruised!" We all, nurse included, began thanking and praising God.

Ten or fifteen minutes later the doctor came in shaking his head. He leaned against the door for a moment before he even spoke and just looked at us. Then he said, "We have X-rayed Rick from head to toe, inside and out. He does not have one broken bone, and no internal injuries!" Again we praised God! That young doctor looked perplexed. He backed away from us and left the room. I'm sure at this point that he decided he had a whole family of "crazies" on his hands.

Rick was taken to ICU where his neurosurgeon informed us he would be at least three weeks. However, the next day he was moved out of ICU into a private room! We were then informed he would be there at least six weeks.

That night as I was standing out in the hall while the nurse checked Rick, a young lady walked up to me, tears streaming down her cheeks. She said, "Mrs. Parker, you don't know me, but I am in college with Rick and I was the person who wheeled him into the emergency room. I would be fired for telling you this, but Rick was dead! We covered him up with a sheet and wrote him off! The doctor was preparing the death certificate when you started the commotion in the hall demanding to see him!"

I told her, "God has given Rick back to us. Isn't that wonderful?"

She replied, "You don't understand, Mrs. Parker, Rick could not live—it is impossible—he was all busted up inside!"

I asked, "Would you like to go in and talk with him?"

"Oh! Can I?" She went inside and talked with Rick for a minute and came out again really crying in earnest! She repeated, "It's impossible—it's impossible! I tell you it's impossible!" I was most happy to explain to her how God specializes in impossibilities! She told me as she was walking away, still crying, "We are all calling Rick our miracle down in the emergency room."

The next night the emergency room attendant came in to see Rick. It turned out that her family had been members of Calvary Tabernacle in Indianapolis, Indiana, for years and she "knew all about Brother and Sister Urshan!" She told me, "You don't really know what God has done for your son. He died on the helicopter and again in the emergency room."

At the time all I could think of saying was, "I know. Isn't God wonderful?"

She also thought I didn't understand. "But you don't understand what a miracle God has performed for Rick—he was dead." She emphasized, "We all thought his neck and back were broken and his brain and insides were all torn up!"

I said, "Pat, I do know. I didn't at that time, but I do know now just what God has done for my son. This is really special to his father and me as we did not ask God to heal Rick—we only asked Him to have His way!"

On Sunday, August 16, the neurosurgeon came to see Rick. After he examined Rick, he turned to me. "Mrs. Parker, we are going to have to operate on Rick's head to stop the spinal fluid leakage. It has been going on too long."

The thought of an operation filled me with a sense of uneasiness, but I felt a surge of renewed faith. I did not know how to respond except to voice my feelings. So I said, "Doctor, God has done the work so far. Please don't talk about operating. God will finish the work!"

Reluctantly, he said, "I'll give you three days and then we must operate."

I will admit that after the doctor left the room, for the first time since the accident, I really felt low. I walked to the hospital chapel and prayed, and as I did, God impressed me strongly to talk with Brother N. A. Urshan, our General Superintendent. I thought this can't be right. I knew that Brother Urshan was ill at the time, and besides, what could he do about Rick's condition?

Returning to the room, I stood at Rick's bedside and prayed all night. On Monday morning I felt even stronger that I should talk with Brother Urshan. I don't pretend to understand how God works, but later that day I did talk with Brother Urshan, and the first thing he said to me, even before I could explain the situation, was, "Don't let them operate on Rick. God has already told me that he will be all right!" I thank God for men who know how to listen to God!

On Tuesday morning they took Rick for three hours of X-rays of his head in preparation for surgery. On Wednesday morning I met the neurosurgeon at the nurse's station. His face was all smiles and he looked very happy. He said, "We don't have to operate! We have discovered that Rick's skull is not 'hair-line' fractured at the base for an inch or so as believed. Rather, his skull is fractured from the top to the bottom and from the middle into his ear. This drainage is mild for that size fracture and it is very rapidly healing itself!" I could only say, "Thank God! Thank God!"

On the morning of August 25, two weeks after the accident, Rick walked out of the hospital, carrying some of his flowers in his hands! At this time, the physical therapist said to us, "Make no mistake, God has performed a mighty miracle for Rick. In the first place, he should not have lived. But since he did survive, he should have been unconscious for six months to one year. After regaining consciousness, he should have received intense therapy for at least two years in Craig Rehabilitation Hospital. Rick is at that point today, **only two weeks after the accident!** You have much to thank God for."

For the final segment of the story, I have asked my son Rick to tell what he remembers.

"I cannot remember having an accident. I don't even remember going to church to work with Dad. The only thing I remember is looking down and seeing Dad and Brother French praying for my body. I was somewhere above them, I don't know where, but I could see everything quite clearly. I could hear them praying and crying. Wherever I was, it was great! I didn't feel any pain. It just felt good and I was comfortable. It was bright, like I was in a great light bright and shining.

"I sincerely thank everyone who prayed for me. I know God has worked a great miracle in my life. I give God all the glory!"

One month to the day, September 10, 1981, the neurosurgeon dismissed Rick and told him he could do anything he felt like doing. He said he really did not know what to tell him as he was not like any other case they had ever had!

My wife and I thank all of you for your prayers and concern for our son. But above all, we thank God for His power and for His mercy He has revealed to us.

NEUROSURGERY

KEITH M. SADLER, M.D., P.C.
JAMES S. OGSBURY, III, M.D.
4200 West Conejos Place
Denver, CO 80204
Phone: 534-3775

October 12, 1981

RE: Richard Parker

TO WHOM IT MAY CONCERN:

The above captioned patient has been under my care for a severe skull fracture and may return to full activity, with no restrictions.

Sincerely,

James S. Ogsbury, M.D.

JSO/eb

October 18, 1981

Mrs. Pat Tulley,
Emergency Room Receptionist
St. Anthony's Hospital
P. O. Box 2245
Denver, Colorado 80201

RE: Richard Wayne Parker
Accident - 8/10/81

Dear Pat:

My wife and I wish to express our deep gratitude for your help and many kindnesses on August 10th, when our son Rick fell off the Church roof.

Your kindness and thoughtfulness meant so very much to us.

Rick starts work again this week. He is again directing our Choir and leading our Song services! We give God all the Glory!

Thank you again for your prayers and many, many kindnesses!

Sincerely,

W. M. Parker,
Pastor

WMP:

Richard before accident.

Richard and family after accident.

CHAPTER FIFTY-SIX

A Miraculous Answer To Prayer

by Isabel Schweiger

God of all emergencies is our God! The dictionary describes an emergency as "an unforeseen combination of circumstances which calls for immediate action."

"Help! Help!" I rounded the corner of Canal street in Trenton, New Jersey and ran right into the distressing cries of a distraught woman. She was hanging out of the second floor window of a high apartment building. Leaning way out of the window she was in an anguish of grief, loudly wailing something in Spanish which I could not understand. Then I saw the man, her husband, dash out of the front door and pick up an object from the sidewalk. It was a baby!

I slammed on my brakes, and jumping out, ran to him. The baby was without a blanket. I knew immediately that it had been thrown from the window above. Looking back I can only explain this certainty that was given to me, as coming from God—the gift of knowledge for that moment. Could a drunken father have done this? No. The man seemed sober, but in a state of frenzied shock. I said, "Give the baby to me," and reached toward it. He gladly surrendered it to me.

"My key! My keys!" he shouted. "I must get my car keys." He raced up the five or six cement steps of the apartment entrance and disappeared. The mother, never letting up her anguished crying, distracted my attention. I tried to get a grip on reality and bring order to my disoriented thoughts. I glanced from her to the baby. I realized the child was turning blue and not breathing. At this moment the father again dashed down the steps and stood before me with a small receiving blanket in his hands. "Go back. Get your keys and bring your wife." I shouted. "Follow me to the hospital!" I didn't know how much English he understood, but I kept repeating "St. Frances Hospital Hamilton Ave." as I ran back to my car and handed the now cyanotic infant to the other woman in the car.

The day had started off serenely enough with the sun shining and pleasant plans for the day. We were not quite finished moving our family of six children back to the shore area of southern New Jersey. We owned a little two-story wooden clapboard house in Somers Point with a pretty woods on one side and the Serfi family on the other.

After spending eight years in the city, I had longed for the shore once more, and so my husband made some needed repairs, and we began to take our belongings, one station wagon load at a time, back to the Somers Point house.

With only a few things remaining, I had asked Mrs. Serfi to go with me to Trenton seventy miles away, and help check the house for belongings before we rented it out. The rest of the day we planned to pick apples in the yard of a friend before returning to the shore.

We had finished our inspection, and gathered up a few things. My husband helped us, and then said "I've got to be going. I'll be late for work." He took a watch out of his pocket and asked, "Could you please take my watch to the jewelers down on State street? I need it badly. The man said he would have it ready tomorrow." I was reluctant to do it. I didn't want to get stuck in downtown traffic. I wanted to pick apples.

He left the house and I debated, "Shall I take it now? Why not wait till we are ready to leave, and drop it off on our way out of the city about four o'clock?"

It seemed really unreasonable and demanding of my husband to ask me to lay aside my plans to run an errand, especially when it interfered with my friend's plans also. However, some ingrained principal guided my decision. "Your husband asked you to do it now," a little voice said.

It was one o'clock! I hastily decided to go. We walked to the side street where my car was parked, and headed around the corner.

Talk about God's timing! It is always perfect! Always right on time!

This was a Pentecostal family, just arrived from Puerto Rico. They did not know a soul. But here comes God's reluctant emissary. Me! The only other Pentecostal in the neighborhood, back for a brief visit, to share this particular moment.

I was praying "Jesus, Jesus," and patting the baby on the back as I slipped behind the wheel and handed him to Mrs. Serfi. She continued my therapy and began calling on Jesus, and patting the baby's back. Mrs. Serfi was a good Baptist, but she did not believe divine healing or miracles were for today.

She was soon to see God perform a miracle. Block after block, horn blowing, pushing through traffic, delay after delay, the baby was still not breathing. Its color worsened each passing minute and it lay limp and seemingly lifeless. Its little head on Mrs. Serfi's shoulder. We were crying and praying, for we expected the child to be declared dead on arrival, or fatally injured. The trip to the hospital, minus traffic delays, would normally take ten minutes. This day we were running out of time.

About a block from the hospital the tiny infant gave a tiny gasp, and began to breathe. It still did not cry, but the blueness faded a little. We began to praise the Lord. Pulling into the emergency entrance we quickly jumped out, and ran into the hospital. I pushed the baby into the arms of the first doctor we met.

"What happened?" he asked.

"We don't know," we answered. "We think it fell, or was thrown from a second story window." Soon a skilled team surrounded the child and first aid measures were administered.

The distraught father arrived shortly afterwards and a Spanish interpreter began asking him questions. Since we were not needed at the hospital, we returned to the child's home. The mother had calmed herself and sat quietly waiting for us. Five or six children were lined up on the sofa like little scared rabbits. We could not communicate because of the language barrier, and I really had no news to tell. But I suggested "Let's pray."

When I got on my knees, they all scrambled to theirs.

At my first word, "Hallelujah," all heaven broke loose as mother and children all raised their voices in the Pentecostal way. We had a grand time with much hugs and smiles afterward. We had wonderful assurance that God had answered prayer.

Going back to the hospital we got a full report. No injury! After careful examination it was discovered that the child had not one broken bone, no fractures, no broken skin, no bruises! It was breathing normally and crying like a healthy baby.

It was later explained to us that the baby was newborn, only four days old. The mother had just brought it home from the hospital that day and laid it on a big bed in the bedroom. While the family was visiting in the kitchen, unnoticed a little two year-old child in the family, feeling hostile toward the new arrival, picked it up, carried it to the open window and dropped it out. The baby hit the concrete steps then bounced to the cement sidewalk.

They kept it for several days under observation. Finally the child was released to the mother with instructions to bring it back every month for a check-up. In two years of monthly examinations, no injury was ever found. Our God answers prayer!

CHAPTER FIFTY-SEVEN

Brought Back From Death

by Mrs. A. H. Browning

On Thursday evening, February 22, 1973, we entertained some guests at dinner. Our friends left and we prepared for bed. Brother Browning, who was recovering from a recent hernia operation, started through the living room to the bedroom. Suddenly he was gripped with an excruciating pain in his chest, arms, and neck. He staggered into the bedroom and asked me to call the doctor.

"Get him to the hospital as quickly as possible," said Dr. Estes when I reached him. Since I had never called the ambulance before in Abilene, it took me some time to get them.

"Hurry or I'll not last until they arrive," Brother Browning urged.

We got him to the hospital shortly before midnight. The next day and night he was hanging in the balance, so to speak. I was allowed to visit him for a short time on Saturday morning.

While I was standing by his bed, he rolled his eyes and his heart completely stopped. Brother Browning said later that he sensed that he was passing from one realm of life to another. The nurses said he was clinically dead.

A young lady from our church went with me into the hospital chapel where we wept and cried in prayer unto God. The chaplain tried to comfort me and told me there were some things worse than death. They were doing their best to prepare me for Brother Browning's passing.

A nurse later informed me that Brother Browning's breathing had stabilized, but I could hardly believe her. Sunday was a bleak day for him. When I visited him on Monday he wrote me a note and said that he did not feel he could make it through Monday night. This so burdened my heart that I went to the waiting room and found several ministers waiting who joined me in prayer again in the chapel. Among them was Brothers John Jones, J. J. Kinsfather, and E. Givins.

At the next visiting hour, Brother Browning said he felt better. On Tuesday he felt that the Lord had spoken to him and that he would make it. He spent sixteen days in intensive care and fifteen more days in the regular hospital. When he was brought home, he was almost helpless. His strength was completely depleted. I had to wait on him as if he were a baby. His recovery was very slow and frustrating to him. As we later visited the hospital and went into the intensive care area, the nurses exclaimed, "Reverend Browning, you are a walking miracle!" There is no question but what God brought him back from death.

CHAPTER FIFTY-EIGHT

A Vision Becomes A Reality

by Mrs. A. H. Browning

In the summer of 1932, I returned from six weeks of summer school at San Marcos State Teachers College at San Marcos, Texas. Since I was getting into the Pentecostal experience, I had returned by the way of San Antonio, Texas, to attend a few nights of revival meeting. I had not yet received the Holy Ghost, nor had I been baptized in Jesus' name. While in San Antonio, I had undergone severe persecution at the hands of my unbelieving sister, who had forcefully brought me back to the home of my parents near San Saba, Texas.

My Aunt Mollie, Mother's sister, had been lying at the point of death for eight weeks with cancer of the stomach. On this day, she was in a bed on the front porch of her home. I was in the house with my mother and one of her other sisters. God had given me a vision of Aunt Mollie being raised up; as I was telling them of my vision, my sister, who is a nurse, came into the room and said, "Aunt Mollie is gone."

As I walked toward the door of the porch, the power of God fell on me. All the family gathered round Aunt Mollie's bed. I then took hold of her hand, life returned, and she raised up praising the Lord, something she had never done before. Her complexion became clear and bright and her beautiful blue eyes shone like stars. She said, "I'm healed, and I want some cake and ice cream."

All those around the bed were sinners without God. They began to cry and call out to God for forgiveness of sins, my mother in particular. My sinful daddy stood with tears streaming down his face. I overheard him the next day tell a neighbor about the wonderful miracle that had happened. As a result of this happening, my mother and two sisters later received the Holy Ghost and were baptized in Jesus' name. Several of my aunts and uncles also received the Holy Ghost.

Aunt Mollie lived until five o'clock the next evening. One of my aunts who was with her said that she raised her hands about thirty minutes before her passing and began to praise and worship God. I believe she was brought back from the regions of death and given something in her soul that she had never had before. To God be the glory.

CHAPTER FIFTY-NINE

God Was Silent No Explanations

by Lorraine Gustafson

"Let's go and see this wonderful place where Jesus lived, Grampa," I pled, as I put my arms around his shoulder and looked at the twinkle in his eyes. Grampa looked over the top of his glasses with a reassuring smile—he knew this five-year-old had fallen in love with Jesus. As he lovingly patted my head, he said, "It would be nice. Maybe, someday. Until then, we will read, talk and dream of being there as we follow Him through the Bible." From that day, one of my favorite wishes was to visit the Holy Land.

When our church announced that they were sending us to the 1980 International Conference in Jerusalem, my heart overflowed with thanksgiving. In "my secret place" I praised the Lord with tears of joy for planning this visit to His hometown, fulfilling another dream of mine to walk where He walked in the country He loved so dearly.

As days crept by and projects were worked on to raise

funds, I began feeling an uneasiness, as though God was not pleased with my going. Again, I resorted to "my secret place" of prayer for His answer. But God was silent. My only answer was the same uneasy, sick convicting feeling that He would not be pleased if I went to Jerusalem. I became frustrated. Why had He changed His mind? Or had I just presumed His approval. Was I ill? Was this the Holy Spirit that I was feeling or my condition? As the time drew near to leave, the feeling became stronger.

That Sunday morning I asked the Lord if it wasn't His will for me to go, to please tell my husband, for he is the head of our home. As is Brother Gustafson's habit, after Sunday dinner and a short nap, he returns to the church to study and pray. As soon as he reached the church that afternoon, he called me. "Babe, I don't know how to tell you this, but I have this definite feeling from God that we must *not* go to the Holy Land at this time."

"Oh, praise the Lord!" I sighed, with complete relief—the depressing feeling gone. "I prayed that the Lord would prepare you and He has."

"He did not tell me why, but we must obey and trust Him for His reason. He knows best," he continued.

We discussed how he would tell the church for they had worked very hard raising money for the trip. We hated to disappoint them. But they understood when we told them. Some felt they should cancel their plans for fear of something going wrong on the trip. We said, "No. If God hasn't dealt with you personally, you will be all right. Perhaps God's just testing us to see if we will obey His leading, even when it hurts. Whatever His reason, we must not fail Him."

The conference was over, our people returned with lovely gifts and told of glorious times in the Lord. But God was silent to us—no explanations.

At the 1981 School of Missions, where I was teaching the children for two weeks, one of the missionaries asked if God had revealed to us why we did not get to attend the Jerusalem conference. "No," I replied, "we haven't the slightest idea. Perhaps we will never know this side of eternity, but we feel good about obeying."

When I arrived home, Brother Gustafson met me at the door waving a letter. "Read this," he said, with a big smile.

"Must be good," I replied, "you're so happy."

It was an invitation from Brother Arlie Enis in West Germany, head of the military district, inviting us to be guest speakers for their Spring Family Retreat in beautiful Berchtesgaden.

Since Brother Gustafson had been in the Air Force when we were married, we knew first hand how needful this ministry was to the military families.

So *this* was God's reason for saying "no" to our trip to the Holy Land. God wanted to share the ministry He had given us with His "dear ones" in the military, protecting our country and others. He had heard their prayers, saw their tears, the lonely night watches, separated from family and friends over long periods of time, enduring many discouragements, often without a pastor to help and advise. He saw their hunger for the Word as Brother Enis arrived for a few days to baptize and instruct like the circuit preacher of old, weary and worn in body but renewed daily in the spirit—traveling on from country to country where our military are stationed. And God's great heart was touched. He began to talk to His children, Brother and Sister Enis, the Foreign Missions Department, the Princeton church and us. He had confidence in all of us to fulfill His long range plans for a retreat for these families.

The economy in our city was very bad at this time. It would have been difficult to raise money for our trip now. God knew the future and planned for us. The church had set aside the funds raised for the Jerusalem trip for us to use at a later date as we saw fit. They were excited and happy to know it was going to be used to minister to our military personnel overseas.

A year and a half after God's definite "no" to Jerusalem, we stepped off the plane in Frankfurt, West Germany. As we drove from the airport we shared these events with the Enises. Our hearts were lifted in praise for the beautiful ways God had led all of us to this retreat. And what a glorious time we had in the Lord with each blessing one another, and God blessing and ministering to all of us—our own personal needs. God had planned this retreat and we were just following His orders, loving His blessings.

I wonder how many beautiful things God has planned for me that I have missed because I ignored His leading and did not wait for His instructions. Therefore, I was not privileged to know His reason and see the workings of His divine plans as they came to completion.

CHAPTER SIXTY

Not on this Side of Eternity

by Ilene K. Dewar

The cool, crisp October day dawned with fresh, brilliant golden rays of sunlight that came streaming across the pale autumn sky. Although the sun gave little warmth, it bravely sent streaks of light to dance off the leaves of brown, yellow, red and green in the woodlands of southern Indiana.

Although it seemed that nothing could penetrate the grief and numbness I was experiencing, these scenic splendors of October 11, 1975, are forever etched in my memory.

The funeral procession moved slowly along the route between the mortuary and the church. Friends and relatives waited at the church to join our family in a memorial service for my dad.

John M. Dewar lived only fifty-three years; the last year of his life was spent in the depths of a coma, suspended between life and death.

Injuries sustained in a traffic accident on September 26, 1974, were responsible for his comatose condition. Very early on that cold, foggy September morning, Dad left the house to go to the store to buy a dozen eggs. About a mile from the house at the intersection of a major highway, an eighteen-wheeler ran a red light at the time Dad entered the intersection driving a lightweight van.

Upon impact, both vehicles made 180 degree turns, the semi-truck, loaded with huge sheets of steel, jackknifed and jumped four lanes of highway. The cab buckled and folded like the bellows of an accordion. The metal sheets were scattered across the highway, damaging portions of the road and forcing the closing of the highway for several hours. Dad's van ended up in a drainage ditch, a total loss.

The driver of the eighteen-wheeler was found wandering along the highway in shock, with a partially severed ear. Dad's injuries were more severe. His head must have struck the windshield before he was thrown from the van. His body skidded along the highway. The bump on his head caused a fractured skull, a concussion and a subdural hematoma. A great amount of pressure was building up inside his head.

While these tragic events were unfolding a mile from our home, we were following our usual morning routine—unaware of how all of our lives were being changed.

My mother and sister were getting dressed for work. I was still sleeping because I was laid off from my factory job. Shortly after my sister left for work, the phone rang; someone listening to a police scanner had heard Dad's name broadcast in connection with a wreck. This man knew Dad and was calling to find out about his condition. We had not yet been informed about the wreck. Mother was frightened. She woke me so I could go find out what had happened. Quickly I dressed and rushed out the door on my way to the scene of the accident. In my mind I pictured a "fender-bender" and maybe minor injuries. I was shocked when I pulled up to the intersection. All I could see was a maze of flashing red lights. Everywhere I looked there were police cars, fire trucks, wreckers and rescue units.

Traffic was beginning to back up now that the rush hour had begun. I parked the car at the side of the road With one glance I saw the twisted wreckage that had been a semi-truck and saw Dad's van nose down in the drainage ditch.

My heart raced wildly and I was dizzy, hot and cold all at once. Somehow I managed to get out of the car and stumble down an embankment to the van where a police officer stood. I identified myself. The officer gave me very sketchy information: (1) my dad was already at Bloomington Hospital, and (2)he only had cuts and bruises. The officer handed me Dad's glasses. There was a crack running lengthwise in one lense and pitted places on both lenses as if small rocks had hit them.

Things around me began to fade away and everything was spinning around. I closed my eyes and almost blacked out, but the officer reached out to steady me. He asked if I needed help to get home. I declined his offer, climbed back up the hill and headed home to break the news to Mom and take her to the hospital.

Mom and I reached the hospital several minutes after my sister. She had already been told the extent of Daddy's injuries and that he probably would not live.

Since Bloomington Hospital did not have either the equipment or the neuro-surgeon to treat injuries like those Dad had sustained, he was transferred to Methodist Hospital in Indianapolis. After diagnostic tests at Methodist, the doctor informed us that surgery was necessary. Without it he would die within hours, but surgery carried no guarantee.

After surgery and for the next week, it seemed that the surgery would save his life although he was still comatose. After one week it again became necessary to operate because another blood clot had formed. We found ourselves in another life and death situation.

After nearly eleven weeks and four neurosurgeries, Dad was discharged to Bloomington Convalescent Center. He was still in a coma. The doctors possessed great skill and knowledge, but they had done all they could do for him. What we needed was a miracle.

I was raised in Pentecost and I believed the stories and messages I had heard on divine healing. As week after week passed with no signs of improvement, we began to despair. I redoubled my efforts in praying for Dad's healing. Preacher after preacher came and anointed him with oil. I knew the only way he would ever regain consciousness and be whole again would be for God to touch him. Weeks became months and on October 8, 1975, just a little over a year from the date of the wreck, Dad died.

After the funeral we came home to an empty house, and I think in that moment my heart was empty, too. I was devoid of despair, but I could not reach out to hope. It was final; Daddy was dead.

I went to my room and stretched out on the bed. Tears

were streaming down my face and, with a heart more broken than it had ever been, I cried out to the Lord.

"Why, Lord, why wasn't he healed? Why did the accident happen and why did he die?"

I reached for my Bible and opened it to a passage of Scripture in Isaiah.

> *"The righteous perisheth, and no man layeth it to heart: and merciful men are taken away, none considering that the righteous is taken away from the evil to come. He shall enter into peace: they shall rest in their beds, each one walking in his uprightness" (Isaiah 57:1-2)*

Then my eyes fell on verse eighteen of the same chapter.

> *"I have seen his ways, and will heal him; I will lead him , also, and restore comforts unto him and to his mourners."*

After reading that final passage, I closed my Bible and with tears coursing down my cheeks, I cried to the Lord. "How can that be, Lord? I don't believe there are any contradictions in Your Word. How can You say You will heal him and then say You will restore comforts to his mourners?"

Then the Lord spoke these words to me: "You asked Me to heal him and I did, but not on this side of eternity."

The miracle of healing did not come to Dad as I wanted it to, but it came as God had planned. The miracle was that a loving heavenly Father took time to bring words of comfort and encouragement to His wounded, broken-hearted child. That comfort has lasted through all the years since Dad's death. What a blessing that once in awhile the Lord lifts the veil just long enough to give us a glimpse into His eternal realm of reasoning.